SACRED & PROFANE
FAITH AND BELIEF IN A SECULAR SOCIETY

Peter Kurti

Connor Court Publishing

CONNOR COURT PUBLISHING PTY LTD
PO Box 7257
Redland Bay QLD 4165
sales@connorcourt.com
www.connorcourtpublishing.com.au

ISBN: 9781922449238 (pbk.)

Cover design by Maria Giordano

Front cover picture: Fireman's funeral, George Street (1894)

Artist: Arthur Streeton

Wikimedia Commons

Printed in Australia

For Scott Cowdell

CONTENTS

FOREWORD
Henry Ergas AO

"Free peoples," wrote Tocqueville in contemplating the America of his day, "have always acknowledged that they find it harder than others to do without religious beliefs." Perhaps, but not in contemporary Australia.

There is, on the contrary, a widespread perception that after decades of decline, the religious faiths on which Australian democracy was founded are doomed to shrink into insignificance, defeated by secularisation's onward march. And as they shrink, the legitimacy of religious voices in the public sphere is increasingly questioned, making people of faith fearful of a future in which their deeply held convictions will be ignored. Nor are those fears misplaced: harassed and harangued by militant secularists who have all the arrogance of hunters who have cornered their prey, Australia's historic faiths are undeniably on the defensive.

Faced with those threats, the risk is that the voice of faith will fall quiet, reduced at best to parroting the fashionable concerns of the day, at worst to resigned silence. Instead, these essays, with their crisp, calm elegance, show that there is an alternative, based on reasoned analysis and respectful deliberation. Informed by careful scholarship and permeated by intellectual honesty, they highlight the contribution faith can make to understanding the issues Australians need to address.

At their core remain the questions Tocqueville posed nearly two centuries ago. "A society," he observed, "can only exist when a great number of men consider a great number of things from the same point of view; when they hold the same opinions upon many subjects, when the same occurrences suggest the same thoughts and impressions to their minds." Nowhere was the need for common ground greater than in democracies, whose passion for equality could all too easily "develop the sentiment of envy to its highest degree," breeding resentment, disrespect for the laws and an ultimately ruinous war of all against all.

How then, Tocqueville asked, "could society escape destruction if, political ties having been loosened, moral ties are not tightened?" It was, he answered, only by relying on widely shared "habits of the heart" which temper self-interest and dissuade citizens from "violating laws that oppose their designs" that democracies could resist the centrifugal forces they unleashed. If the nascent American republic succeeded in that respect it was because, "while the law permits the Americans to do what they please, religion prevents them from conceiving, and forbids them to commit, what is rash or unjust."

There was, he concluded, a foundational complementarity between religion and freedom. "Religion regards civil liberty as a noble exercise of men's faculties, the world of politics being a sphere intended by the Creator for the free play of intelligence;" at the same time, "Freedom sees religion as the companion of its struggles and triumphs, the cradle of its infancy, and the divine source of its rights." Shorn of that mutual support, democracy's inherently conflictual nature would make freedom increasingly unbearable; as a result, while "some religious peoples may have been enslaved, no irreligious people has remained free."

All that may seem extraordinarily distant from Australia's current circumstances. But, as Peter Kurti lucidly shows, the transformation of what was once the common ground of a society in which spiritual concerns mattered into the fractured terrain of a society which lacks any stable sense of moral authority has eroded not only our ability to work together but also the tolerance and mutual respect that is indispensable if we are to live together. Far from making for greater liberty, the weakening of moral authority has undermined the civility on which the viability of a free society rests.

To say that is not to pine for a mythical golden age of consensus. Democracy is not about eliminating cleavages and divisions; rather, its genius lies in converting adversaries into rivals, making what might have been a battle field into a playing field. But that is only possible if there are agreed rules of the game, with none of those rules being more important than that which recognises the legitimacy of each of the participants.

It is that legitimacy, as an accepted participant in the democratic process, which the secularists refuse to accord to religious faith. To make matters worse, while the secularists may scorn belief in God, they have certainly not abandoned their belief in the devil. And Christianity and even Judaism increasingly figure as the demon they seek to exorcise out of public life.

No one would claim that those efforts will destroy Australian democracy; but if they are allowed to succeed, they will certainly impoverish it, depriving it of voices that deserve to be heard, reducing its standing with a large share of the population and making it an even harsher, more rancorous place than it now is. Already today, as these essays demonstrate, that process is well underway, degrading the public debate on issues that range from the so-called 'right to death' to the emergence, this time on the political left, of the cancer of anti-Semitism.

We owe the word, 'religion', to the Latin, 'religare', which means to bind or to tie back. In the Roman mind, to be religious meant to be tied to the past, not by refusing change but by grasping the present's duty to the inheritance it had received from previous generations and its obligation faithfully to discharge that duty for the benefit of the future. It was in that context that the word 'authority', or 'auctoritas', originally appeared, not as a synonym for power but as what might almost be viewed as its antithesis. Power, 'potestas', was the ability to control; 'auctoritas', derived from the verb 'augere', was the ability to augment, and what was to be augmented was precisely the legacy that had been left by those who ran the city to their successors, and which they now held in trust. Authority was therefore intimately linked to responsibility, and to have authority was to be answerable to an unbroken chain that united what was, what had been and what was to be.

The West's political tradition built, however imperfectly, on those foundations; they are, of course, long gone, replaced by an eternal 'now' that lacks any defining sense of its antecedents and its posterity. To believe that what has been lost could be restored would be absurd; but it would be every bit as foolish to gloss over the costs and consequences of our loss. By exploring today's issues in the light of reason and tradition, these essays teach us that and more, making them a resource to be read, admired, and enjoyed.

INTRODUCTION

MORAL CHOICE IN SECULAR SOCIETY

In a democracy the state is neither with us nor against us. It is us. This is why most of us are so ambivalent about it. But our collective expectations depend for their fulfilment on its persistent intervention in almost every area of our lives.[1]

In the first months of 2020, sudden expansion of the powers of the state caused widespread concern as many countries imposed strict lockdowns in response to the coronavirus pandemic. Confinement to the home and limits to movement outside the home were some of the measures imposed in open, liberal societies.

These restrictions were, at first, accompanied by zealous police enforcement. This, in turn, raised concerns about the status of civil liberties long taken for granted in countries such as Australia. People feared the first shoots of an emergent police state. Many governments were also keen to use tracing apps in mobile phones to track progression of the virus. As a result, concerns about privacy, about intrusiveness of the state, and about the permanence of measures said to be temporary, and therefore justified by circumstances, continued to mount.

Debate about how to strike a balance between protection of public health and protection of privacy became heated.[2] Many measures intended to combat the spread of COVID-19 did, indeed, prompt significant questions about the

1

relationship between the citizen and the state. In exceptional circumstances, civil freedoms were, with consent of the people, circumscribed by government. This dramatic imposition of limits on individual liberty nonetheless served as a reminder of the need for the citizen to remain vigilant about exercise of state power.

Political obligations arising in the relationship between state and citizen came under particular scrutiny during the pandemic. Authority of the state is one part of the equation; obligations and rights to which citizenship give rise are another. At the same time, it is important to balance a commitment to individual liberty with the overall well-being of the community. Indeed, when the common good is at issue – especially in a major public health crisis which has serious economic consequences that result directly from government action – it may be necessary for the liberty of the individual to take second place.

Proponents of classical liberalism can frequently place such a premium on the liberty of the individual that they overlook the importance of these social institutions and communal bonds. In the broad terms espoused by such thinkers as Adam Smith and Edmund Burke, however, classical liberalism has always balanced the rights of the individual against the duties and obligations owed by the citizen to the wider community.

A commitment to personal freedom, therefore, needs to be tempered by a recognition that human beings are social animals and that our relationships to one another form a web of mutually owed duties and responsibilities. As such, the role of citizen is also more complex than a purely transactional account according to which the citizen has certain rights that it is the duty of the state to protect.

Our relationships with others, and with wider society, are mediated through the network of voluntary, civic associations – Edmund Burke's "little platoons" – that comprise civil society. These associations include, primarily, the family, but also community organisations, religious institutions, charities, sports teams, cultural and artistic societies, and trades unions. Each plays a role in building civic trust and holding to account those who exercise political power in the state.

A strong civil society affords effective protection from arbitrary and capricious government. Where the institutions and relationships that comprise civil society are absent, nothing remains to mediate the relationship between the individual citizen and the state. Where community withers, social, cultural, and economic prosperity decline, too.

Responsible citizenship must, therefore, embrace the vital importance of community to the health of society. There may be times, as in a pandemic, when it is necessary to accept the need for timely and appropriate constraints upon individual liberty when needed to preserve that health. But failure of the institutions of civil society will, soon enough, threaten the liberty enjoyed by all citizens.

All the essays in this collection were written before the 2020 coronavirus pandemic. But, in one way or another, at the heart of each one lies the matter of this compact between citizen and state, and the importance of free participation in the collective life of the community on equal terms that we may pursue our individual lives on fair terms with others.

These 'equal terms' are not principally concerned with wealth or levels of income; they are, instead, concerned with civic rights and duties, with standing before the law, and with opportunities for social and political participation. Equality thereby expresses the idea of shared interest and mutual obligation, fundamental components of what ancient Greek democracy called *isonomia*, and what we might call, simply, *citizenship*.

This conception of citizenship, characterised by equality and openness, is a key feature of societies that are often collectively identified as 'the West', a term that occurs frequently in this collection of essays. The civilisational roots of the West are traced by scholars such as Larry Siedentop and Rodney Stark to theological conceptions of the individual expressed in the Judeo-Christian tradition dating from the 1st century CE. Historians, such as Paul Collins, trace those roots to the period of the 10th century CE when early modern systems of government and jurisprudence began to evolve in forms recognisable to us today.[3]

The West expresses far more than a geographical grouping of countries. It is preferable to think of it as an idea which bears characteristics and principles informing the collective life of many societies around the world – some of which, such as Australia, are far removed geographically from other societies standing in a similar tradition. The source of the West's evolutionary power has been, as noted by Bill Emmott, a former editor of *The Economist*, "its openness, its equality of rights, and so its social trust."[4]

These distinguishing features are essential for enabling societies in the West to maintain social cohesion even as they become increasingly multicultural and continue to integrate those from non-Western societies. Another crucial factor, helping to promote social cohesion as levels of religious diversity increase, is the secular character of the Western state. A recurring theme in these essays is the importance of reconciling an individual's religious identity with her status as a citizen of a secular state.

'Secular' denotes, broadly, the non-religious domain in which politics is concerned with the affairs of this world and not of the next. The citizen with religious beliefs, however, will often have concerns that do transcend the temporal realm and demand the freedom to advocate for policies whose principles are consistent with her faith tradition. Human sexuality and euthanasia mark two of the great contemporary points of divide between secular and religious outlooks in the West. Many religious people regard secular views about sexuality and physician-assisted suicide as signs of the world's alienation from God, and they demand the freedom both to say so, and to act upon that conviction. Their non-religious opponents object vigorously to this stance.

If one distinguishing feature of the West is its capacity to forge cohesion from diversity, however, the citizen with religious beliefs must be as free as any other to contribute to debates about policy and law. The evolving shape and character of a liberal democratic state ought to be of concern to every citizen, and the secular status of the state must not be a ground for excluding the voice of the citizen with religious beliefs.

These questions, bundled together in the topic of religious freedom, remain important in the West where many services to society – such as in education, health care, and aged care – are provided by faith-based organisations whose religious principles necessarily inform their work. Reconciling the right of citizens with religious beliefs not to be unduly burdened in the free exercise of religion with the need to govern on behalf of – and for the well-being of – all members of society remains a thorny challenge for governments in the secular states of the West.

Each of the essays in this book examines one or more dimensions of this challenge and looks at how the secular state might strike an appropriate balance between the needs, beliefs, and concerns of all its citizens, both those who hold religious beliefs and those who do not. They have their origin in a series of reports written and published in the course of my work at the Centre for Independent Studies in Sydney but have been rewritten and edited to be more accessible to a general readership. They are intended to be read in any order, and no essay presupposes that any of the others has been read beforehand.

The first chapter, *Cracking Up? Culture and the displacement of virtue*, argues for restoration of the language of virtue in public discourse to address what many consider to be the crisis of moral authority confronting secular societies. This crisis has arisen, in part, because of the subjective turn in society away from the communal to the personal. This turn is represented by widespread use of the language of values. Whereas values are subjective and can only describe emotional, felt experiences of the individual, virtues appeal to an objective standard that express communal, shared norms of morality, locating them in the wider frame of a common human nature.

The second chapter, *Religion and the ethics of citizenship in a secular society*, examines questions and antagonisms arising in the search for an accommodation between the needs of religious citizens and the demands of citizenship in a secular society. It is the only essay in this collection not previously to have been published and was written for a forthcoming *Festschrift* in honour of Adjunct Professor J. R. Nethercote of the Australian Catholic University. I am grateful to the editors of the Festschrift, Professors J.J. Pincus and Henry Ergas, for permission to publish the essay here first.

Another examination of religious diversity in a secular society is attempted in chapter three, *A shy hope in the mind*, this time from the perspective of the economics of religion. A leading figure in the field is Laurence Iannaccone whose supply-side analysis of the 'religious economy' and religious behaviour discloses far more vitality than critics of religion often care to admit. Accounts of secular society that overlook the significance of religion are, almost certainly, bound to be misleading and ill-informed.

The fourth chapter surveys three of the principal religious roots of Western civilization. *Reason, Repentance, and the Individual*, originally delivered as the Robert Iles Memorial Lecture in Adelaide in 2017. In identifying these three roots, the essay seeks to underline the importance of the West's religious heritage and to argue that they are foundational to the secularism that characterises Western civilization.

The next two chapters, *Dying with dignity*, and *Dignity: a poor reason to legalise assisted suicide,* can usefully be read together and they arose from my interest in arguments surrounding advocacy for the legalisation of physician-assisted suicide, or *voluntary assisted dying*, as its proponents prefer to describe it (misleadingly). The essays argue that pre-approving suicide is antithetical to the very notion of human dignity and involves a rejection of the social and communal obligations human beings owe one another. Nonetheless, demand for the legalisation of physician-assisted suicide continues to grow in many Western countries, including Australia. *Dying with dignity* is a revised version of an article that first appeared in *Quadrant* (July/August 2016); *Dignity* first appeared as an article published in volume 6, issue 2, of the *Griffith Journal of Law and Human Dignity* in 2018. I am grateful to the editors of these journals for permission to reproduce these essays here.

One hoary objection to religion, frequently mounted by its critics, is that it is a principal progenitor of violence. Acts of terrorism perpetrated in the name of Islam have only fuelled this objection. The seventh essay, *Terror in the name of God*, examines the nature of religious violence and asks whether those who kill really do so in the name of God, or whether they are simply actors who are identifiable as followers of that god. Secular Western societies, having embraced religious pluralism, take no position on claims made by faiths about what is true or good. Yet religious violence confronts those societies with rejection of that very pluralism by a group of citizens whose place in society has depended upon it.

Antisemitism is another form of religious violence although one that extends beyond boundaries defined by religion itself. The final essay in this collection, *Anti-Zionism and the postmodern Left*, examines a particular manifestation of antisemitism on the political left which purports to be nothing more than moral and political criticism directed at the policies and actions of the State of Israel. The scandal of antisemitism that has dogged the British Labour Party, and its former leader, was the most egregious recent instance of this form of hatred; but it is present on the political left in other countries, including Australia. The essay urges those on the left, long-committed to pursuing justice and human decency, to free itself of the ugly taint of this ancient hatred.

REFERENCES

[1] Jonathan Sumption, *The Trials of the State: Law and the Decline of Politics* (London: Profile Books, 2019), Kindle edition, location 209.

[2] Rebecca Gredley, "Phone tracking the next step in virus battle", *Australian Financial Review* (15 April 2020), See also, "COVID-19, surveillance, and the threat to your rights", Amnesty International (3 April 2020).

[3] See, Paul Collins, *The Birth of the West* (New York: PublicAffairs, 2013).

[4] Bill Emmott, *The Fate of the West* (London: Profile Books, 2017), 7.

1

CRACKING UP?
Culture and the displacement of virtue

Culture is properly described not as having its origin in curiosity, but as having its origin in the love of perfection; it is a study of perfection.[1]

There is growing anxiety that, in Australia, something has changed for the worse in our culture. The change is perceptible but often defies precise description; yet it provokes unease in many quarters because of a concern that the foundations upon which our common social life is lived have become unstable.

The kinds of change that have given rise to this general, pervasive restlessness about the health of the culture are familiar enough. They include a sense that common bonds of civility that help to build mutual trust are under strain.

Norms and principles of social life that prevailed as recently as a decade ago have been upended and many – especially those of conservative disposition – feel that this happened suddenly and unexpectedly. They are left with feelings that things they value are no longer of value to others.

The experience of cultural change that has occurred frequently provokes a widespread and persistent apprehension among the more conservatively minded, that the warp and weft of the social fabric have altered – that the culture is broken – and in ways that are often discomfiting and unsettling.

This sense of cultural displacement is one of a number of important factors that account for the rise of nationalist-populism, and of the challenge it poses to mainstream politics. As Roger Eatwell and Matthew Goodwin have argued, supporters of populists are driven by a desire to restore to the political agenda a broader set of principles and "to reassert cherished and rooted national identities over rootless and diffuse transnational ones."[2]

What has happened to the culture?

Defenders of such change contend that the culture is not broken at all, but is responding to evolving sensitivities and understanding. And, indeed, an increased awareness of the need to combat behaviours that discriminate on the grounds of race or gender is one example of 'good' cultural change that has occurred during the past fifty or more years.

Many are concerned, however, that this cultural evolution has not stopped with the correction of aberrant behaviours. The assertion of rights has been weaponised and anti-discrimination laws are increasingly used to stifle expression of opinion, often but not necessarily conservative, rather than simply combat bad behaviour.[3] This is nowhere more evident than in the tension between religious belief and sexual identity.

The Morrison Government's introduction of a series of bills to address religious discrimination late in 2019 is an example. The Religious Discrimination Bill, in particular, proposes that discrimination on grounds of religion should be made unlawful; it also creates a new post of Religious Freedom Commissioner in the Australian Human Rights Commission. The bill will establish religion as a protected category just as race and sexuality are already protected categories.

Will the ALP (Labor) support the passage of this bill through the Parliament? It remains to be seen. At the time of writing (November 2019), the Attorney-General, Christian Porter, was still inviting community responses to the bill.

Even though religious freedom featured prominently in the 2019 election campaign, Labor is still likely to be wedged by the Greens. The Greens' position is that any measures to bolster religious freedom are nothing less than "a barefaced attempt to write a blank cheque to discriminate against LGBTI [lesbian, gay, bisexual, transgender, intersex] people."[4]

This tension is an example of cultural shift, marked by two related features. The first feature of cultural shift is a move away from the communal — and, with it, a diminishing civic readiness to live with difference — towards the individual, and a concomitant demand that threats posed by difference must be eradicated so that any behaviour deemed to harm individual dignity be proscribed by law.

The second feature of cultural shift is related to this emphasis on the sensitivities of the individual. Emphasis on the primacy of the individual away from the communal is evident in eclipse of the moral language of virtue by the language of values. And this is important because, as this essay will outline, values language cannot successfully serve as a language of morals.

As a consequence of the cultivation of virtue having given way to the expression of values, when defenders of cultural change engage with those who resist it, their exchanges are invariably passionate and ardent because they are committed to a notion of the primacy of individual and personal dignity.

The term, 'culture', itself, is a term tossed about casually enough; but often without attention to what it is and why it matters. Given that 'culture' has a complex range of meanings, it is important to clarify what is actually meant when considering culture before addressing the failure of virtue.

Culture and the social unconscious

The term, 'culture', can refer to a body of artistic work as well as to a process of intellectual and social development. 'Culture' can also refer to the whole set of principles and practices by which a community of individuals lives and works – whether in a household, a profession, an institution, or an organisation. The definition of culture given by the *Oxford English Dictionary* sets appropriately the context for the discussion:

> The distinctive ideas, customs, social behaviour, products, or way of life of a particular nation, society, people, or period. Hence: a society or group characterised by such customs.[5]

Culture thus refers to the broad social and moral context within which a society functions. It is about a whole way of ordering life; like the air we breathe, culture can be taken for granted. But we ignore the health of the culture at our peril, and therefore need to be vigilant about safeguarding it.

This is why efforts to reform a culture inevitably require more than mere compliance with whatever regulatory and legal frameworks are imposed by governments. Keeping to the letter of the law is one thing; changing an entire moral approach to standards of life is quite another.

According to literary critic Terry Eagleton[6], a significant component of culture that emerges from the *OED* definition is that of the social unconscious. This is derived from Wittgenstein's account of 'forms of life' in which a great deal is assumed or taken for granted. 'Culture' represents the collective summation of the customs, beliefs, and symbolic practices by which people live in a society.[7]

In Eagleton's view, culture can be both intensely self-aware, but also a good deal less so: "In [this] latter sense, it constitutes the invisible colour of everyday life, the taken-for-granted texture of workaday existence, too close to the eyeball to be fully objectified."[8] Culture as "the invisible colour of everyday life" echoes Edmund Burke's notion of the resemblances, conformities, and sympathies that bind a community of common interests.

According to Burke, whom Eagleton thinks of as the finest exponent of the idea of culture as social consciousness, sensitivity to culture involves "studying the genius, the temper, the manners of the people, and adapting to them the laws that we establish."[9] For Burke, culture is more fundamental than law or politics: it is "the matrix of all power, contract, authority, and legality. Culture is the sediment in which power settles and takes root."[10]

This account of culture as 'sediment' affords a priority to culture as the sphere of life within which all other forms of life and activity are pursued. It is to this extent that culture is a manifestation of the social unconscious. It is a view often expressed in the aphorism, favoured by conservatives, that *politics is downstream from culture.*

Burke's notion of a commonality of interests serves as a critical component of the social contract that enables the legitimate and constitutional exercise of governmental power and authority. The limits of what is possible in politics are described by the broader cultural context in which the activity of politics takes place. Healthy political authority can only flourish through a sensitivity to culture that can be understood as an intricate mesh of affinities and observances.

One area of the broader cultural context in which political activity takes place is the sphere comprised of the practices of trade and commerce, the expression of public opinion, the work of the media, the administration of justice, and the liberty of the citizen. This sphere is often referred to as 'civil society'; the arena of social conduct, the health and character of which is governed by shared beliefs and behavioural norms. According to Francis Fukuyama[11], the political scientist, civil society is "the realm of spontaneously created social structures separate from the state that underlie democratic political institutions."[12]

Civil society is constituted by what Fukuyama describes as "precursors and preconditions" lying at the deeper level of culture, which he defines as "a rational, ethical habit passed on through tradition."[13] Civil society is, therefore, informed by that Burkean 'sediment' of culture in which it takes root; it is shaped, in turn, by the habits, decisions, and traditions of a people:

> Culture, broadly understood, is the riverbed of politics, setting the course along which it flows. But that course is checked and channelled by wilful human activity – by building dams and canals, as it were.[14]

The sediment of culture, however, comprises more than the rational and ethical dimensions of virtue. It embraces sentiments and emotions; such as feelings of reverence, attachment, and devotion that cannot necessarily be expressed in terms of reason. Therefore, to some extent, the sediment of culture is pre-linguistic and pre-rational; for it includes among its components the felt experiences of a people.[15]

In some respects assumptions made about the consistency and uniformity of that riverbed of politics have been challenged by the emergence of 'cultural diversity' as a force in political and social change.

Cultural diversity – with political manifestation in the form of multiculturalism – is a factor that can function as a shield to protect the practices and beliefs of minorities from the predations of the majority; but it is now wielded just as readily as a sword by, or on behalf of, minorities to enforce acceptance of those practices and beliefs by the majority. Sometimes affirmation of those practices may contravene society's laws or norms, or both. The practices and beliefs arising in Islam that affect the rights of women, such as the wearing of head coverings, are an example of this.[16]

Multi-cultures?

Australia's official policy of multiculturalism commenced in the 1970s during the Whitlam Government (1972-1975). It was intended to foster a spirit of respect and tolerance by addressing forms of social exclusion thought to have been experienced by migrants and their descendants arriving under the country's post-war immigration program. This policy approach of the 1970s was partly motivated by a well-intentioned desire to rid the country of what many considered to be the stain of the White Australia policy.

The White Australia policy was established in 1901 but dismantled in stages by the Menzies and Holt governments after the end of World War II, between 1949 and 1966; an early conspicuous example was the adoption of the Columbo Plan in 1950. In that period, programs of multi-ethnic migration were developed to encourage non-British and non-white immigration.

The *Migration Act 1966*, passed by the Holt Government, effectively ended the White Australia policy by greatly increasing access of non-European migrants. Ten years later, the Whitlam Government adopted measures to prevent race being considered a factor in shaping immigration policy, and passed the *Racial Discrimination Act* in 1975, making all forms of racially-based selection unlawful.[17]

Nearly half a century later, multiculturalism is no longer simply a response to diversity. It is now the means of regulating it. It does so by treating society as a collection of separate ethnic groups that are dependent upon government-managed responses to diversity.[18] The origins of this latter development can be traced to that period of legal and social reform when, as political scientist Kenneth Minogue[19] has noted, "the doctrine of tolerance began to make claims about reality, and turned into the belief that all cultures are of equal value."[20]

In Minogue's opinion, these claims about reality have given rise to imposition of what he describes as "a dictatorship of virtue imposed upon a previously free people."[21] This determination to identify and defend the rights both of individuals and various self-identifying 'victim' groups has now hardened into an oppositional confrontation between competing groups, each of which tends to deny it has any obligations to any other group.

Multiculturalism challenges assumptions about the extent to which any single culture can be considered to be shared and held in common. As such, culture has become a contested arena in which factors of equality and power are considered to be both important and formative. As these factors have been 'weaponised', so the dictatorship of virtue has become far less tolerant of individual freedoms of speech, religion, and conscience when the exercise of those freedoms is deemed to offend or harm dignity. This mounting intolerance, characteristic of a fetish of diversity, poses a grave threat to the health of the culture.[22]

Notwithstanding the questions that multiculturalism raises about the existence of a multiplicity of cultures coexisting within a society, the term, 'culture', nonetheless is still able to convey a sense of the depth of the soil within which diverse convictions, beliefs, and practices common to a society are rooted.

Indeed, as anthropologist Adam Kuper[23] has argued, the differences between people in a given society arise from what is shared; and what is shared depends on our inter-relationships. In emphasising this point, Kuper invokes Claude Levi-Strauss's dictum that: "Diversity is less a function of the isolation of groups than of the relationships which unite them."[24]

Uncertainty about the strength or resilience of the relationships that bind us in the diversity of our common life explains current concerns about the direction of Australia's culture. This sense of cultural de-alignment, spreading rapidly now through Australian institutions such as universities and commercial corporations, serves only to intensify concerns that the fabric of civil society – and in turn, the health of our democracy – is fragmenting.[25]

Culture and democracy

Recall that culture is the context within which any particular social form of life emerges and grows. However, the social form with which this discussion is concerned is specifically that of a liberal democracy.

In broad terms, 'democracy' can be understood as referring to a method of collective decision-making in which all participants in that process enjoy equal status. A 'liberal' democracy is one that promotes liberty by encouraging active political participation of citizens by means of voting; and where the rule of law and the exercise of established freedoms serve as limits to the scope of government.[26]

Liberal democracy is, in the view of political scientist Robert Audi[27], characterised by two fundamental commitments. First, there is a commitment to the freedom of citizens, upheld both by the rule of law and by obligations assumed under international treaties and conventions. Hence, democracy is characterised as *liberal*. Second, there is a commitment to the political *equality* of those citizens, which is commonly epitomised in the practice of equal voting rights, often referred to in Australia as 'one vote, one value'. Thus, the autonomy and the political rights of citizens are to be respected in a liberal democracy:

> A vote can represent a citizen's political will only if it is autonomous. This entails that it is not only uncoerced but also free of the kinds of manipulation and rights violations that would prevent its appropriately representing the values of the voter.[28]

A society comprised of participants who enjoy both freedom and equality will be marked by diversity of belief, ideology, and morality. Hence, when the collective arrives at a decision, it is always possible that the views of some will prevail and the views of others will not. Differences of morality and world-view can thereby pose a significant challenge for the life of a liberal, multicultural society.

How might this challenge of diversity best be met? One response is to hold that in a plural democracy, where different sets of values and different lives can combine in many varied ways, it is never possible to justify the assertion of one set of moral principles over another. This view holds that the justifiability of moral values is always relative and there are no universal normative standards. Moral judgment is, accordingly, always relative both to culture and to circumstance.

For critics such as Eagleton, by contrast, cultural relativism is "a vastly implausible position" that must be rejected. Cultural relativism holds that any idea that human existence rests upon universal foundations is illusory and that it is culture, itself, that is foundational. Yet Eagleton also argues that culture is not foundational, either:

> To see everything as relative to culture is to turn culture itself into an absolute. It is now culture that one cannot dig beneath, as it used to be God or nature or the self. Culture is not identical with our nature, as the culturalists claim; rather it is *of* our nature. [Italics in original][29]

Eagleton is surely correct that human nature precedes culture, and that culture gives expression to – perhaps *emerges from* – human nature. If human nature is accepted as foundational for culture, the expressions of different beliefs and practices encountered in a multicultural society characterised by diversity must not be mistaken for the co-existence of different cultures. For critics such as Eagleton, therefore, 'multicultural diversity' must rest upon a presumed shared foundation that underpins such diversity of expression.

Eagleton seems to think of this shared foundation as a kind of human universal into which specific attributes of different cultures are absorbed. But, as the bonds of civil society diminish, and the claims of one group are asserted against those of another, presumptions about the existence of such a shared, universal foundation weaken and falter. This is what gives rise to apprehension about the capacity of a broader (and deeper) culture to be a valid expression of a human universal.

Culture and moral authority

Sociologist Philip Rieff[30] is one commentator who has advanced prescient warnings about the weakening of a shared foundation and its impact on culture. For Rieff, culture has a *moral* component, in that it describes the moral demands that inform and shape human behaviour. Rieff understands culture to be based on a shared vision of ideal moral behaviour, especially the kinds of behaviour that are forbidden or taboo.

Many activities and behaviours are possible for human beings; but, according to Rieff, it is culture that imposes the restraints on individual behaviour necessary for upholding moral and social norms. Without these restraints, human beings would slip into what he describes, poetically, as the "abyss of possibility."[31] Rieff argues it is culture that allows human beings to acquire a sense of meaning and purpose, an argument noted by Jerry Muller, an historian of ideas:

> By attaching the self to some larger set of shared goals, and by requiring that man's [sic] asocial or evil urges be repressed or redirected towards higher, ultimate purposes, culture provides individual purpose and collective cohesion.[32]

The historian, John Hirst[33], used the term, "bedrock principles", to characterise the set of shared goals essential for a diverse, pluralist society. According to Hirst, these principles are to "guide our society and allow us to resolve our differences and to live with those differences which cannot and should not be resolved."[34]

The process by which these bedrock principles, together with a sense of purpose and cohesion, are internalised by the individual is *education*. The family was considered by Rieff to be the most important educational institution for fostering cultural awareness; but more formal education institutions such as schools and universities – and those who staff them – also have an essential role in developing an awareness of the moral limitations of possibility in children and young people.

Muller notes Rieff's warning that: "where intellectuals regard their mission primarily as the opening up of possibilities rather than recalling the reasons why possibilities ought to be foreclosed, they pave the way for barbarism."[35] In other words, without a moral framework for deciding which possibilities it is appropriate to pursue, the individual runs the risk of choosing any possibility that is open. For Rieff, to choose like this is to tumble into the limitlessness of the abyss.

John Hirst

The 'bedrock principles' are to guide our society and allow us to resolve our differences and to live with those differences which cannot and should not be resolved.

Rieff's particular contribution to discussion about concerns for the development – or deterioration – of culture emerges from his detailed criticism of Freudian psychoanalysis and the consequent emergence of what he describes as "the culture of the therapeutic."

In his view, psychoanalysis has contributed to the erosion of inherited cultural norms and helped to create a human being committed solely to the cultivation and tending of the inner life.

Muller explains that Rieff was critical of psychoanalysis because, in retaining an openness to as many options for living as possible, the 'therapeutic' type is thereby schooled against commitments that are binding or permanent:

> The bottom line of every social contract was the escape clause. This applied not only to personal commitments but to cultural or intellectual commitments as well. Commitment itself was viewed as a form of therapeutic self-enhancement, with each commitment to be abandoned when self-enhancement diminished.[36]

Commitments liable to be abandoned include religious and moral precepts inculcated by family, school, and community. The abandonment of commitment, in turn, leads to a further weakening of a shared moral sensibility, and the consequent questioning of other forms of restraint and authority. As Muller notes, Rieff attributes much responsibility for these developments to the activities of intellectuals:

> Abandoning their traditional role of articulating the necessity of the repression of desire for the sake of communal purposes and higher authority, intellectuals [are] increasingly devoted to demonstrating the arbitrariness of all restraints and authority.[37]

Rieff's warnings about the emergence of the 'therapeutic' individual who is committed to little more than their own self-enhancement have proved prescient in many ways. Reasoned argument has, indeed, given way to an emotivist preoccupation with the individual's own feelings and experiences; and intellectual elites have been in the vanguard of this development.

The eclipse of religious and moral codes of conduct that provided authoritative boundaries of restraint and self-control has been one factor contributing to the weakening of community cohesion. The quest for salvation of the soul has given way to a yearning for fulfilment of the self that stands apart from communities bound together by common beliefs.

In weighing the prescience of Rieff's analysis, sociologist Lauren Langman[38] laments the prevalence of hedonism in contemporary culture – what he describes as "the amusement society" – and regrets what he considers the unrestrained pursuit of "feeling good":

> In our current 'amusement society', an essential moment of a 'therapeutic culture' oriented to feeling good, we see that gratifying images have supplanted complex thought, that political and intellectual discourse now consists of sound bites, sight bites, jingles and platitudes.[39]

Rieff sounded early warnings both about the imminent deterioration of culture – marked by a heightened priority given to the autonomous preferences and experiences of the individual – and also about the weakening of the rational and emotional bonds and obligations arising in community that bind members of a society together.

Just such changes in culture are evident in contemporary Western societies like Australia, where there is an evident shift in emphasis away from the communal – as represented by a general commitment to a society's bedrock principles and a willingness to live with difference – towards the individual; with the concomitant demand, asserted in terms of the politics of identity, for the imposition of restrictions on any speech or conduct alleged to diminish recognition and respect.

This shift is particularly apparent in the way the personal has taken primacy over the communal, and in the way the cultivation of virtue has given way to the expression of values.

From virtues to values

Whether referring to the classical virtues of the Ancients, or the theological virtues of the Christian era, the concept of virtue has functioned as the bedrock for the good life of individuals and the well-being of the state.

The 'cardinal' virtues celebrated by Aristotle were: wisdom, justice, temperance, and courage. They were supplemented by prudence, magnanimity, munificence, liberality, and gentleness. The 'theological' virtues are: faith, hope, and charity.

Virtues are objective moral norms that are both shared and personal. They are shared because there is general agreement about what the virtues are and what they represent; and they are personal because once an individual knows what the virtues are, they can make a personal evaluation about how they stand in relation to any particular virtue.

As morality became increasingly relativised and subjectified in the 20th century, however, the language of 'virtues', which asserts a degree of objective authority based on a shared human nature, gave way to the language of 'values' as a moral language. For historian Gertrude Himmelfarb[40], this change in language from virtues to values meant the resolute character of moral claims, formerly afforded a sense of authority based on the idea of virtue, weakened:

> One cannot say of virtues, as one can of values, that anyone's virtues are as good as anyone else's, or that everyone has a right to his [sic] own virtues. Only values can lay that claim to moral equality and neutrality.[41]

It is assumed that values refer to something objectively real or factual; they assert, however, only a subjective, aesthetic assessment of worth, the expression of personal preference, which is unverifiable by facts and without any basis in tradition or social consensus.

As such, values are simply emotional statements about personal beliefs, feelings or attitudes. They cannot be normative because it is impossible to erect any shared meaning on the foundation of something that is personal and subjective, a point well made by the Australian legal scholar, Iain Benson:

> Since 'values language' is, at best, ambiguous, and at worst, inherently relativistic, it is actually opposed to a

language that could further notions of objective goodness and shared meanings. This is why it is the enemy of character, citizenship and culture all of which, in some part, depend on shared understandings to develop well.[42]

It is because values are a subjective assessment of worth that they cannot impose any moral obligations on others — even though we may want them to mean something in a shared way. "The language of value," according to the Canadian philosopher, George Grant,[43] "is what is left once you have eliminated the idea that there are purposes that intrinsically belong to being."[44]

The problem is that what is left does not amount to much. This has serious implications for the way we think about virtues as determinative, authoritative standards of behaviour that express a shared moral purpose grounded in a common nature and supported by tradition and social consensus.

Whereas the language of virtues requires that we conform to what is obligatory and shared and good, the language of values leaves us with nothing about which we can agree. This is compounded by the fact that arguments about acceptable standards of civil behaviour are fuelled by emotion — that is, by *feelings* about one's own status and that of others.

The emotivism that drives confrontation undermines any sense of reciprocal obligation which undermines, in turn, a sense of shared belonging. But without such a sense of shared belonging, there can be none of the moral obligation essential for the effective recognition and upholding of rights.

Rights and obligations

As already noted, the drive to define and defend the rights of individuals was originally prompted by a determination to be inclusive. This was the motivation for reform of human rights law in Australia which has won legal protections against discrimination on the grounds of race, sexual orientation, gender, and disability.

Appeals to human rights entail the demand that universally valid standards of behaviour are always recognised, and that certain forms of behaviour are open to reasoned criticism and reform. As such, the defence of human rights and freedoms depends on a foundation of reason.

But those earlier reforms prompted by sound, moral motives have given way to conflict between those who advance the relative merits of varying claims; and as Paul Collier, an economist, has recently noted, "the resulting oppositional identities are lethal for generosity, trust, and co-operation" — all of which are essential for social cohesion.[45] If rights are to be asserted, they must always be tethered to a sense of obligations owed.

A commitment to human rights is, after all, founded on certain widely accepted assumptions about human beings and the way they should live. Yet emotion has displaced reason, and rights have turned into demands for acceptance and affirmation. Reasoned thought gives way to hurt feelings; and emotion, rather than reason, serves as the new basis on which claims against others are asserted.

Displacement of reason by emotion is already having a significant impact on contemporary debates in Australia about the balancing of different rights claims. For example, the right to recognition and affirmation claimed by transgendered people is now asserted with such vigour that the questioning of transgenderism is both unwise and tendentious.[46] Restrictions such as these pose a serious threat to the fundamental right to freedom of speech — even on a university campus, where open enquiry, assumed to be an essential feature of academic discourse, is now constrained.[47] Questions about the right to religious liberty were raised during the debate in Australia about same-sex marriage in 2017: would those with a faith-based objection to same-sex marriage be compelled either to endorse or to conduct marriage ceremonies that were contrary to the tenets of faith?

Notwithstanding a review of religious freedom led by Philip Ruddock, a Liberal politician and former Commonwealth Attorney-General, the Morrison Government has yet to implement any reforms to uphold religious liberty.[48] Legislated protections were expected to be in place by the end of 2019. In the absence of action by the Government, religious believers have been understandably apprehensive that the advance of some rights — especially concerning sexual orientation — will continue to threaten the free exercise of religion in Australia.[49]

Believers base their calls to protect religious liberty on their reasoned understanding of what constitutes a good society in which the rights of all citizens are respected equally under the law. But their appeal to reason may well fail as our fixed points of meaning, based on reason, are being replaced by emotion.

Thus, religious institutions currently campaigning for legal protection against discrimination on grounds of religion are likely to find that the ground of reason upon which they were confidently building their arguments has shifted. Failing to notice this tectonic movement, the campaigners will continue to build; but, like a foolish person, they will be building on sand.

Reasoned discourse about rights and obligations becomes impossible if we discard the language of virtues and resort to values language. Rights lie beyond mere choice and preference, a point made well by Iain Benson:

> If we believe moral beliefs to be relative, then we cannot have a commitment to 'justice' shared by all global communities and we would not be able to subscribe to the main concepts in *The Universal Declaration of Human Rights* (1948). These are not 'universal values' because there are, in fact, no such things. 'Values language' rejects the idea of shared moral goods as essential and necessary.[50]

Rejection of "shared moral goods" takes us very far from

the Burkean understanding of culture as the sediment in which the institutions of civil society are rooted. The shift from virtues to values also removes us far from the notion that culture is a habit — or series of habits — passed from one generation to another, as advanced by Fukuyama.

The series of habits broadly comprising Western culture were at one time committed to upholding the principal rights and freedoms of all citizens as the mark of a liberal democracy. Increasingly, however, those rights have been displaced in the name of diversity. Liberties enjoyed equally by all have been subverted in pursuit of protections for the dignity, emotions, and feelings of a few.

Culture after virtue?

Once values displace virtues, the idea of a shared morality soon loses any coherence or meaning — even in the face of authoritarian assertions that such a shared morality exists. Claims using the language of morality purport to go beyond expression of personal preference and to appeal to a standard that transcends personal preference and experience.

But while the language of morality may continue in use in the age of emotion, moral claims made using that language will mean something quite different because they do not, in fact, refer to virtues at all; they refer, instead, to values. Thus, the statement that 'This is good or bad' can mean no more than 'This is what I choose to approve or disapprove.'

A statement that merely expresses a personal choice may certainly be passed off — and often is — as a statement of objective truth binding on all members of society. Even if that statement may come to have legal force, it can have no inherent moral force despite protestations to the contrary by the proponents of values.

Appeal to a transcendent, authoritative standard can make sense only within a broader community in which such standards are both acknowledged *and* shared. In some societies, the common moral authority might be religious;

but a society could accept a common moral authority without that authority taking a religious form. The extent to whether such standards are either acknowledged or shared in contemporary culture is, however, very uncertain.

Once virtues give way to values, and reason to emotion, it is not just common standards of behaviour that erode quickly. Without a broad consensus about the way things are done or the rules to be followed, the very language we use in civil and moral discourse begins to fragment and, soon enough, loses its meaning. It was on this basis that the philosopher, Alasdair MacIntyre[51], observed some fifty years ago that the notion of moral authority was no longer viable:

> For the notion of authority can only find application in a community in which there is an agreed way of doing things, according to accepted rules. An agreed right way of doing things is logically prior to the acceptance of authority as to how to do things. Unless there is an established and shared right way of doing things, so that we have social agreement on how to follow the rules and legislate about them, the notion of authority in morals is empty.[52]

The nature of contemporary discourse in the public square, concerning such topics as those identified earlier, suggests MacIntyre was correct in pronouncing the non-viability of the notion of a common authority. If so, the notion of culture as a series of universal, transmissible, collective customs, beliefs, and sympathies is no longer viable either.

Politics, conservatism, and the 'culture wars'

Concern about the viability of culture as a series of transmissible customs has had a serious impact on the political life of Australia as a gulf widens between those on either side of the political divide. It is certain to affect the sphere of practices and behaviours, and the realm of contractual and voluntary relationships that comprise civil society. And this, in turn, is going to have — some would say is *already* having — a profound impact on our long-term capacity to bind into a cohesive whole the variegated communities and individuals that, together, have forged Australia into a prosperous, integrated, and multicultural society.

The conduct of public debate has been coarsening steadily, however. The tone of political exchange has become increasingly shrill as arguments about energy, climate, refugees, agriculture, and water increasingly make appeals to personal feelings of grievance, guilt, and shame —rather than to reason, evidence, and duty.

The implications of this corrosion have been especially pressing for the centre-right side of politics in Australia. There is a concern, voiced most notably and forcibly by the journalist, Paul Kelly[53], that conservatism in Australia appears to have lost the capacity to articulate clearly the key moral principles which should underlie public policy. This loss has occurred at a time of heightened moralism in politics on the part of those on the Left.

Kelly argues that conservatives' reticence about the moral dimension of policy, and consistent failure to bind issues of morality and politics together, has led to them struggling, over a period of a decade or more, to shape public opinion effectively. In this failure, conservatives have missed the changing spirit of the times — the *zeitgeist*. Kelly tellingly observes:

> The political impact of the *zeitgeist* cannot be missed. There is nothing as vulnerable as an idea targeted by the progressive forces; witness traditional marriage, coal, and tax cuts for corporates. And there is nothing so resilient as a failed idea to which the progressive class is attached; witness open borders, wage rises divorced from productivity, and government intervention as a superior allocation mechanism to markets.[54]

Whether it is climate change, immigration, fiscal policy,

gender identity, or freedom of speech, Kelly argues that the Left was skilful in coupling debate about policy to debate about morality. Wisdom accepted in an earlier age appeared, today, to be rejected; policy acceptable to an earlier generation of voters appeared to be ideologically unfashionable to a new one. Thus, consideration of key moral principles — such as equality, fairness, duty, responsibility, and compassion — were always integral to formulation of policy on the Left.

It was feared that these developments would contribute to the detected long-term erosion of support at the ballot box for conservative governments deemed by the electorate to be unpersuasive, confused, and disconnected.

Paul Kelly

The political impact of the zeitgeist cannot be missed. There is nothing as vulnerable as an idea targeted by the progressive forces; witness traditional marriage, coal, and tax cuts for corporates. And there is nothing so resilient as a failed idea to which the progressive class is attached; witness open borders, wage rises divorced from productivity, and government intervention as a superior allocation mechanism to markets.

With the country preparing to go to the polls in a Federal election in May 2019, Kelly was concerned that the advantage apparently enjoyed by those on the Left of Australian politics was due, in large part, to an ability to frame every significant policy issue in clear and comprehensible terms that appeal to a sense of a collective morality.

Certainly, Kelly's warnings about a crisis facing Australian conservatism appeared to be borne out in successive opinion polls that predicted defeat for the Coalition at the 2019 Federal election. In the event, fears about such a defeat were not realised, and the Coalition was returned to office with a very slight majority, and more seats than it had before the election.

Commentators poured over this unexpected Coalition victory. A broad theme that emerged quickly was that the Australian Labor Party and its leadership had engaged in a degree of moral over-reach, exaggerating claims about lack of fairness and growing social and economic inequality. This argument was expressed succinctly in an editorial in *The Australian*:

> Labor recklessly reprised class war, anti-market rhetoric, redistribution and big government. This is Australia in sepia, clueless, in defeat. Labor disowned its proudest legacy [the Hawke-Keating reforms of the 1980s and 1990s] by insisting on a story of national failure. That didn't sit well with a people whose material living standards have doubled in the past 50 years.[55]

All the same, it remains to be seen how the Coalition's 2019 election victory will affect this admittedly bleak scenario. The forces of identity politics have long been on the march in Australia; and many were expecting those forces to gather momentum under a Labor government. In preaching a transformative moral vision for the country, however, the political Left appears to have badly misjudged the character of the Australian voter.

For example, that ideological, moral vision ridiculed and

dismissed the views of those 66 per cent of Australians who declared a religious affiliation in the last census. Had it been brought to fruition, it would have threatened to traduce the ethos of religious institutions by removing long-standing exemptions afforded under anti-discrimination laws. This would have prevented institutions such as schools, hospitals, and aged care facilities from upholding the tenets of their faith.

The election results also indicate that unease about the diminished role of moral language in articulation of centre-right policy was misplaced. The apparent advantage that Kelly felt the Left had acquired because of its appeal to a collective morality appears to have evaporated.

It is unlikely the Morrison Government will, in the short to medium term, attempt to adopt the interventionist and redistributist policies advocated by the Left while retaining a conventionally conservative approach to the economic challenge of boosting prosperity and building productivity. Senator Amanda Stoker is one parliamentarian who has exposed emphatically the falsity of this dichotomy.[56]

Stoker, in the lead-up to the 2019 Federal election, argued that it is simply not open to conservatives to yield any ground to the progressives who seek to tribalise society along lines of race, gender, or religion.[57] This would amount to a betrayal of the conservative, classical liberal principles that have been the bedrock of Australian prosperity since the Second World War. She argued that social and cultural issues are inseparable from those that are economic and fiscal.

Stoker contends that reclaiming a voice for conservatism must begin with a debate about the role of government and other institutions in the life of the citizen. This entails reaffirming the importance of individual responsibility and, with it, the principle of individual liberty:

> We must start talking about freedom to people who don't know, or have forgotten, that getting to a better place in life can, and should, start with taking control of one's

life. [This involves] taking back control, [and] owning the decisions that come with freedom, along with their consequences.[58]

The pressing question is whether conservatism in Australia can make up this lost ground in what is frequently described as the 'culture wars'. For Stoker, sitting on the sidelines of debates about the moral dimension of politics is not an option for conservatives, because it simply cedes the public square to political opponents who would shape the debate.

To wage the culture wars with any hope of success, it is essential to understand how the forces of the Left have changed the contours of the culture by emphasising the primacy of identity over community, and of the preferences of the individual over the needs of the communal.

Why defending culture matters

In *Culture and Anarchy*, the 19th century essayist, Matthew Arnold, argued that the true value of culture lay in its being an indispensable aid to the fullest realisation of the human spirit.

Arnold declared that culture "moves by the force, not merely or primarily of the scientific passion for pure knowledge, but also of the moral and social passion for doing good."[59] For Arnold, culture was the pursuit of perfection and the means of getting to know the best in all matters that have contributed to human flourishing. In this pursuit of perfection, therefore, Arnold is clear that culture combines both moral and social elements.

The argument presented in this essay is that the fracturing of our culture can be accounted for, in large part, by the crisis of moral authority that confronts our society. The eclipse of virtue by values has led to a distorted view of morality that is no longer informed by principles of reason but by emotion. The communal norms of morality expressed by virtue have been displaced by a new primacy afforded to feelings.

Senator Amanda Stoker

We must start talking about freedom to people who don't know, or have forgotten, that getting to a better place in life can, and should, start with taking control of one's life. [This involves] taking back control, [and] owning the decisions that come with freedom, along with their consequences.

The fissures in our culture can be closed only by a reinstatement of a moral authority that appeals to norms that transcend the felt concerns and experiences of the individual, and instead locates them in the wider frame of a common human nature so that all may flourish. This must be done, in other words, by appealing to virtue. Yet this is no easy task.

The language of morality in the West is regarded by many with suspicion. Indeed, arguments against positions advanced by the Left, and framed, as such, in terms of appeals to conservative conceptions of moral authority, are frequently met with scepticism, at best, and derision, at worst — dismissed as ideology and 'hate-filled' bigotry. We see this repeatedly in debates about issues such as climate change, gender, school curricula, and the family. It accounts for the assertion of safety as an assumed moral good in its own right.

While acknowledging the formative influence of religion on the development of Western moral thought, it must be stated clearly and unequivocally that the argument is not about the restoration of any form of morality determined solely by the demands of theology or institutions of religion — whether Christian, Muslim, Jewish, or any other.[60]

What it calls for is a renewed understanding of culture as that which expresses a shared, common vision for our human and social flourishing — an understanding passed on in our traditions to future generations. Only in this way can culture, in Arnold's sense of the pursuit of perfection, give meaning to human experience.

The prevalence of a largely 'change for the sake of change' progressive agenda in contemporary discourse will continue to present a challenge to those committed to pursuit of this vision of human flourishing. Yet, committed to that vision, conservatism can also affirm that human flourishing depends, in turn, on recognition and protection of fundamental human rights and freedoms — including the right to liberty in religion, not as a subordinate right but as one right coexisting with other rights.

As such, the crisis of moral authority confronting our society poses a substantial threat to religious liberty. This crisis should be addressed by, first of all, refusing to accept equation of emotional claims with moral claims, and by calling for a reorientation from the personal to the communal. The moral, social, and political health of our society — indeed, of our culture — depends upon it.

REFERENCES

1   Matthew Arnold, *Culture and Anarchy* (Oxford: OUP, 2009), 34.

2   Roger Eatwell and Matthew Goodwin, *National Populism: The Revolt against Liberal Democracy* (Pelican: London, 2018), xxxii.

3   See, for example, Stephen Chavura, "It's the word police who threaten harm", *The Australian* (28 May 2019); and James Taranto, "What went wrong with human rights?", *The Wall Street Journal* (17 August 2018).

4   See Paul Kelly, "Labor faces key test in religious discrimination bill", *The Australian* (5 June 2019).

5   *Oxford English Dictionary* (online edition).

6   Terry Eagleton (b. 1943) is a British Marxist critic and literary theorist currently based at the University of Lancaster.

7   This is one of several working definitions of "culture" offered by Eagleton in Terry Eagleton, *Culture* (Yale University Press: New Haven CT, 2016).

8   Terry Eagleton, *Culture* (Yale University Press: New Haven CT, 2016), 50.

9   Quoted in Terry Eagleton, as above, 62.

10 Quoted in Terry Eagleton, as above, 64.

11 Francis Fukuyama (b. 1952) is an American political scientist and political economist based at Stanford University in the United States of America. His most famous book is *The End of History and The Last Man* published in 1992.

12 Francis Fukuyama, "The Primacy of Culture", *Journal of Democracy*, Vol. 6 No. 1 (January 1995), 8.

13 Francis Fukuyama, as above, 8.

14 Daniel McCarthy, "A New Conservative Agenda", *First Things* (March 2019).

15 I am grateful to Dr Michael Casey for clarifying the distinction between the rational and emotional components of culture.

16 See further, Peter Kurti, *The Tyranny of Tolerance: Threats to Religious Liberty in Australia* (Connor Court: Redland Bay QLD, 2017), 61 et seq.

17 See Peter Kurti, as above, 49 et seq.

18 Peter Kurti, as above, 59.

19 Kenneth Minogue (1930 – 2013) was an Australian political scientist who spent much of his career at the London School of Economics. His last book was *The Servile Mind*, published in 2010.

20 Kenneth Minogue, "Multiculturalism: A Dictatorship of Virtue", in Patrick West, *The Poverty of Multiculturalism* (Civitas: London, 2005), vii.

21 Kenneth Minogue, as above.

22 See Peter Kurti, as above, 97.

23 Adam Kuper (b. 1941) is a South African anthropologist whose particular interest in social anthropology has led him to investigate the functions of culture.

24 Adam Kuper, *Culture: The Anthropologists' Account* (Harvard University Press: Cambridge, Mass., 1999), 243.

25 For further analysis of the pursuit of cultural diversity in Australian commercial life, see Jeremy Sammut, *Corporate Virtue Signalling: How to Stop Big Business from Meddling in Politics* (Connor Court: Redland Bay, QLD, 2019).

26 See Roger Eatwell and Matthew Goodwin, as above, 83.

27 Robert Audi (b. 1941) is an American philosopher and political scientist with a particular interest in the role of religion in politics.

28 Robert Audi, "Moral Foundations of Liberal Democracy: Secular Reasons and Liberal Neutrality toward the Good", *Notre Dame Journal of Law, Ethics, and Public Policy*, Vol. 19 (2005), 197-218, 198.

29 Terry Eagleton, as above, 42-43.

30 Philip Rieff (1922 – 2006) was an American sociologist and cultural critic who spent much of his career at the University of Pennsylvania.

31 See the introduction to Rieff's thought in Jerry Z. Muller (ed.), *Conservatism: An Anthology of Social and Political Thought from David Hume to the Present* (Princeton University Press: Princeton, NJ, 1997), 411.

32 Jerry Z. Muller (ed.), as above, 412.

33 John Hirst (1942 – 2016) was an Australian historian and social commentator who worked for much of his career at La Trobe University in Melbourne.

34 John Hirst, *A Republican Manifesto* (Oxford University Press: Melbourne, 1994), 19.

35 Jerry Z. Muller (ed.), as above, 412.

36 Jerry Z. Muller (ed.), as above, 413-14.

37 Jerry Z. Muller (ed.), as above, 414.

38 Lauren Langman is an American sociologist and social theorist based at Loyola University Chicago in the United States.

39 Lauren Langman, "Philip Rieff's Mission: Character, Culture, and Morality", *Journal of Classical Sociology*, Vol. 3:3 (2003), 279-295, 289.

40 Gertrude Himmelfarb (1922-2019) was an American intellectual historian known in particular for her research on the Victorian era in Great Britain.

41 Gertrude Himmelfarb, *The De-moralization of Society: From Victorian Virtues to Modern Values* (IEA: London, 1995), 12.

42 Iain T. Benson, "Do 'values' mean anything at all? Implications for law, eduction and society" *Journal for Juridical Science*, (2008) Volume 33 (1), 1-22, 7,8. Benson also developed this argument at greater length in his 2017 Acton Lecture delivered at the Centre for Independent Studies and later published as, Iain T. Benson, *Civic Virtues and the Politics of 'Full Drift Ahead'* (Centre for Independent Studies: Sydney, 2017).

43 George Grant (1918-1988) was a Canadian philosopher and political commentator whose best known work is *Lament for a Nation*, published in 1965.

44 Quoted in Iain Benson, "Values Language: A Cuckoo's Egg or Useful Moral Framework", in David Daintree (ed.), *Creative Subversion: The Liberal Arts and Human Educational Fulfilment* (Connor Court: Redland Bay, QLD, 2018), 11.

45 Paul Collier, *The Future of Capitalism: Facing the New Anxieties* (Allen Lane: London, 2018), 59.

46 Any such questioning needs to be raised with care. In response to controversy about transgender inclusion in sport, for example, the International Olympics Committee has recently committed to fund research into the matter; but the research was said to pertain to "injury and illness prevention". See Dawn Ennis, "IOC to fund research of transgender athletes", Outsports.com (13 March 2019). I am grateful to Simon Cowan for drawing this to my attention.

47 James Carmody, "UWA cancels talk by transgender sceptic Quentin Van Meter after protests", ABC News (18 August 2018).

48 In November 2017, Ruddock was invited by the then Prime Minister, Malcolm Turnbull, to chair a review of religious freedoms in Australia following the postal survey on same-sex marriage. The report was delivered in May 2018.

49 See, for example, Nicola Berkovic, "Religious freedom bill fails to meet election deadline, *The Australian* (10 April 2019).

50 Iain Benson, as above, 28, footnote 33.

51 Alasdair MacIntyre (b. 1929) is a British philosopher whose principal work has been in moral and political philosophy. He has worked at numerous British and American universities. He is best known for his important book, *After Virtue*, published in 1981.

52 Alasdair MacIntyre, *Secularization and Moral Change* (Oxford University Press: London, 1967), 53.

53 Paul Kelly (b. 1947) is an Australian political journalist and author, and Editor-at-Large on *The Australian*.

54 Paul Kelly, "Culture shift points to political change", *The Australian* (16 March 2019).

55 Editorial, "The secret, simple genius of Australian democracy", *The Australian* (21 May 2019).

56 Amanda Stoker (b. 1982) has been a Liberal member of the Commonwealth Senate representing Queensland since March 2018.

57 Amanda Stoker, *Taking Back Control: Restoring Universalism in the Age of Identity Politics* (Centre for Independent Studies: Sydney NSW, 2019).

58 Amanda Stoker, as above.

59 Matthew Arnold, *Culture and Anarchy* (Oxford University Press: Oxford, 2006), 34.

60 On the importance of secular government in Western liberal democracies, see further, Roger Scruton, *Where We Are: The State of Britain Now* (Bloomsbury: London 2017).

2

RELIGION AND THE ETHICS OF CITIZENSHIP IN A SECULAR SOCIETY

*Modern liberal societies are heirs to the moral confusion
left by the disappearance of a shared religious horizon.*[1]

Secularism and religious freedom in Australia

Religion has become front page news in Australia.[2] Findings
handed down at the end of 2017 by a Royal Commissioner
investigating allegations of sexual abuse of children are only
part of the story; but they, alone, have done much both to
catch the attention of the wider public and to diminish the
social and moral standing of religious institutions here.[3]

There are other factors explaining renewed contemporary
interest in religion. One is Islam's increasing influence
in Western countries, including Australia, along with
conflict generated by radicalised fundamentalist forms
of Islam. Another is the mounting challenge to religious
freedom posed by attempts, often made with disconcerting
vigour, to exclude religion as a protected category in anti-
discrimination legislation.

A broader culture war against religion is being waged
in Australia. This war has inflamed arguments about the
appropriate place, if any, that religion should occupy in

formation of public policy in Australia's secular liberal democracy. Whereas contemporary discussions about diversity in Australia focus, for the most part, on race, gender, and sexual orientation, however, they also need to embrace the religious diversity of our multicultural population.

Respect for diversity must not give way to the strictures of identity politics that elevate the notional rights of a group above those of the individual. The danger posed by identity politics is that diversity can become a source of social division and the diminution of liberty. Diversity needs always to be tempered by the rule of law.

At the outset, a brief survey of two recent key issues that have provoked this renewed debate – same-sex marriage and the charitable status of religious not-for-profit organisations – will help to put some loose folds of flesh on the argument to be developed.

Fuelled by distaste for religion in any form, self-styled social progressives have thereby helped to keep it in the news by their determination to eliminate any public expression of religion, or any influence that it might have, in society. The problem, as identified by these advocates, can be stated succinctly: in a diverse society such as Australia, it is highly likely there will always be a substantial proportion of the population that finds any religious argument or reason for a policy unacceptable.

Is it not, therefore, reasonable to argue that the only acceptable grounds for public policy in a secular liberal democracy should be secular ones, and that religious grounds cannot ever be relied upon to advance public policy? It is a contention that defenders of religious liberty need to answer.

This debate is the product of a rising tide of secularism, something different from the increasing secularization of society. *Secularisation* is the process a society goes through as its attachment to religion diminishes.

Secularism, however, refers less to a diminishing concern for the religious than to a conscious process of actively, even aggressively, promoting the secular. Hence, the *Oxford English Dictionary* defines "secularism" as: "the view that religion and religious considerations should be deliberately omitted from temporal affairs."[4]

Since a policy of deliberate omission can take different forms, the term, 'secular', can be used in elliptical ways. In terms of the formulation of public policy, a more precise definition of a policy ground or reason as 'secular' has been offered by Robert Audi[5], a political scientist:

> [A] secular reason [is] one whose normative force, that is, its status as a *prima facie* justificatory element, does not depend on the existence of God (or on denying it) or on theological considerations, or on the pronouncement of a person or institution *qua* religious authority.[6]

In the hands of the more aggressive proponents of secularism, an absence of justificatory dependence on God (or the Bible) is often elevated to a concerted effort to banish altogether any element of religious influence, in any circumstance, from the public sphere.

This essay will examine the relationship between the religious and the secular by examining the underlying principles at stake in a plural society. Quite often attacks are not directed at religion in itself, but at any argument which can be said to have a religious origin or rationale. Forcible exclusion of religion amounts to a betrayal of the underlying principle of neutrality which ought to inform a properly secular society in which faith and public life are reconciled.

Far from excluding and marginalising citizens with religious beliefs and inspirations, the secular liberal state should aspire to embrace the principles of individuality and diversity, and to protect those principles by the imposition of procedural and legal limits on what the state can do. The liberal order, in other words, stands for peace through toleration, and for liberty protected by the rule of law.

Threats: no place for 'meddling' believers?

Same-sex marriage

Urgency to pass legislation amending the *Marriage Act 1961* mounted swiftly following declaration of the results of the Australian same-sex marriage survey on 15 November 2017.[7] The result of the postal survey had been decisive, and amendments to the Act were passed by the Commonwealth Parliament on 7 December 2017, little more than three weeks later.

There were concerns about the haste with which the amendments were passed. The editorial writer of *The Australian* considered the Government's "poor preparation and lukewarm commitment to freedom of religion, conscience, and belief" had led to a legislative outcome that appeared to brush aside concerns held by many Australians about the strength of religious protections.[8]

A sizable minority of respondents to the postal survey – 40 per cent – were opposed, in some cases, on religious grounds, to any change in the law. Commentators, such as Richard Ackland, a columnist, argued that this losing minority is simply not entitled to demand legal provisions to protect their freedoms of speech, conscience, or religion:

> There are strong grounds for a campaign to counter the expansion of religious freedoms and to reduce the ones that already exist. When you consider the hateful, cruel, bitter, and downright false contribution of religious voices during the recent survey, why would anyone want to give these institutions more open-ended 'freedoms'? There is a long and sorry history of churches meddling in society's freedoms and undermining citizens' human rights and private lives.[9]

Arguments such as these, based exclusively on the perceived – and acknowledged – failings of the Christian church, hardly do justice to the cultural and religious diversity which is so characteristic of Australia's thriving multicultural society. This is a diversity reflected in successive returns for the Census conducted by the Australian Bureau of Statistics every ten years.[10]

Charitable purpose

Religion contributes to Australian society in ways beyond the practices of individual believers. Many charities, or not-for-profits (NFPs), functioning in Australia today, for example, either remain, or were in their early days, Christian organisations, such as the St Vincent de Paul Society and the Benevolent Society.[11]

The charitable purpose of advancing religion has been part of the English Common Law tradition for more than 400 years. The preamble to the *Charitable Uses Act 1601 (England)*, also known as the *Statute of Elizabeth*, influenced the judgment in a late 19th century case, *Commissioners for Special Purposes of Income Tax v Pemsel* [1891], which established four heads of charitable purposes including "the advancement of religion".

While the definition of charity and the heads of charitable purposes have been amended by the Commonwealth Parliament, charity law in Australia still follows English Common Law closely. The *Statute of Elizabeth* and *Pemsel* continue to influence Australian courts.[12]

This legal tradition, together with the well-established presence of faith-based not-for-profits in Australia, has not deterred a recent move by a member of the Legislative Council of Victoria, Fiona Patten, to attempt to amend that state's *Charities Act 1978* to exclude the advancement of religion as a charitable purpose. According to Patten (who formed the Australian Sex Party in 2009):

> The notion that the advancement of religion is a charitable purpose would be questioned by most people in our community these days. I don't believe that the community thinks that advancement of religion is a charitable purpose.[13]

Patten does not substantiate her belief with any evidence as to the precise views of people in the community. Underlying her rhetoric, it might be reasonably supposed, is a determination to check the capacity of religious not-for-profits – including healthcare, welfare, and aged-care agencies – to influence the formation of law and public policy.

Responses: religion assumes the discourse of politics

Nearly forty years ago, in BBC Reith Lectures delivered in 1978 and speaking specifically about Christianity, Edward Norman, an English ecclesiastical historian, warned of the dangers of what he called "the politicization of Christianity". He feared that this process was, in part, a symptom of spiritual decay.

This decay, Norman argued, was not the consequence of an assault by the enemies of religion; it was due, instead, to the surrender by Church leaders of Christianity's claims to an understanding of the nature of humankind:

> Christians have adopted the moralities of secular political ideologies and promote them for what they think of as authentically Christian social ends. They are redefining their own moral identity and their own claim to significance in society in terms of an external context dominated by ideologies which have no other end for man [sic] in prospect except as part of the material process.[14]

When conflicts do arise between religious people and organisations, they are now more likely to be about sharply defined political beliefs as they are to be about points of theology. Some religious people and organisations, clearly, now hold that politics does not so much involve a choice between reasonable alternatives but assertion of self-evident moral truths.

Anxious about marginalisation of religion in public life, some religious organisations in Australia have responded by adapting their stance on key political issues of the day and altering the ideological basis of their contributions. In other words, they seek to influence formation of public policy by substituting the more acceptable modes of secular discourse for the discourse of theology.

Religious bodies such as the National Council of Churches in Australia (NCCA), for example, frequently take positions on social and economic issues by attempting to recast the propositions of theology as unvarying secular, moral principles. Thus, in November 2016, the NCCA endorsed the international COP22 Interfaith Climate Statement.[15] According to an accompanying media release, this statement, signed by 304 religious leaders from 58 countries, declared, among other things, that the continued use of fossil fuels is ethically untenable and called for "shifting public finances away from fossil fuels, increasing financing to end energy poverty with renewable energy, and ensuring a just transition that protects human rights and vulnerable communities."[16]

The Statement, itself, was cast wholly in secular, humanist terms which appealed to general principles of justice, moral obligation, and the duties of "trustees to Mother Earth."[17] Mention of God, if made at all, was scarce. When even religious organisations abandon the language of theology, the process of secularization may be said to be well advanced.

Secularization has marginalised religion. One consequence is that some religious people stake their ground in secular social discourse, expressing their endorsement or rebuttal of political policies by means of the language of justice and rights. This ideological switch is one development characteristic of the settlement developed in most liberal democracies between the religious and the secular.

The secular settlement and the primacy of individual autonomy

Arguments that religion can never, in any circumstances, inform the development of public policy in a secular liberal democracy reflect significant changes that have occurred in the attitude of Western culture to religious belief.

One change often cited to account for this displacement of religion, and the diminution of the prestige and power of religious institutions, is the complex process of the modernisation of society, together with progress made in science and technology.

According to this view, empirical methodologies and their accounts of causal explanation have rendered metaphysical world-views redundant. Religion, in turn, has become restricted to overseeing the means of salvation and, as a result, has also become far more individualised.

Steve Bruce[18], a sociologist, traces these changes to the Protestant Reformation of the 16th century which also played a major part in laying the foundations of liberal democracy:

> What were initially religious arguments inadvertently encouraged individualism, egalitarianism, and diversity, which in turn combined with growing and structural differentiation to shift governments in the direction of secular liberal democracy.[19]

Yet just as the status of Christianity in modernising liberal democracies has changed, so, too, sizeable non-Christian religions have emerged in the West since the 1960s, in large part due to changing patterns of migration. Many migrants came from countries more religious than their new homes in the West; the immediate impact of this has been to increase the public visibility – if not the acceptance – of religion in the West.

This has not, however, stemmed the tide of secularisation, a process widely regarded as irreversible – unless a reversal of the increasing cultural autonomy of the individual is conceivable. "Unless we can imagine some social forces that will lead us to give up that freedom, we cannot imagine the creation of a detailed ideological consensus."[20]

The primacy of individual autonomy is a key component of the classical tradition of the 'secular settlement' developed by liberal democracies. There are two principal elements of this settlement. The first is that the private and public spheres of life are to be clearly demarcated. The religious beliefs and practices of the individual are tolerated in the private sphere, but not in the wider public sphere where all religion is excluded.

The second element of the settlement is that religious bodies such as schools, hospitals, and welfare agencies, are permitted to retain certain privileges – such as exemption from some anti-discrimination laws, and certain tax advantages – on condition that they do not rock the social, political, and cultural boat.

Indeed, the threat in Victoria to deny religion as a charitable purpose, and withdraw from it certain long-standing exemptions, referred to earlier, suggests that religion, at least in the minds of some, is doing too much rocking of society's boat already.

Threats to the secular settlement

This secular settlement works so long as those seeking accommodation are tolerant of all others. In some circumstances, however, the settlement comes under threat. Thus, if a minority – whether religious or anti-religious – rejects the principle of demarcation between the private and public spheres, and seeks to impose law or policy on the tolerant majority, such action will threaten the liberties of those with whom the dissident minority does not agree.

For example, when same-sex marriage activists urge removal of anti-discrimination exemptions from religious groups committed to a traditional form of marriage, they effectively seek to impose their views and beliefs on those with whom they disagree.

The settlement will also be destabilized when a minority seeks to do something in private that offends against a principle shared by the wider society. For example, the desire by some Muslim women in Australia to wear the *niqab*, or some other form of Islamic veil, in public places, is frequently resisted by non-Muslims because it is said to offend tenets fundamental to a secular liberal society, such as the equal status of women.

Demands, such as these, for the public privileging of religion have, in the opinion of scholars such as Steve Bruce, helped to provoke antagonism towards religion. This has been driven, in part, by the increased presence in secular societies of non-Christians, such as Muslims, who have not been party to the gradual evolution of the demarcation of private and public spheres.

Indeed, this troublesome public presence of religion might serve to confirm, rather than reverse, the privatisation of religion and so strengthen liberal commitments to the secular settlement.[21] In addition, Bruce is sceptical that concerns about the marginalization of religion are shared by members of wider secular society:

> To the extent that some Christians now behave like a disadvantaged minority and make a fuss about their rights, they simply confirm the view of the secular, or only nominally Christian majority, that religion is more trouble than it is worth.[22]

Secular protagonists certainly often depict religious argument in very blunt terms. Their caricatures of religion present it as it were little more than "a crude prescription from God, backed up with threat of hellfire, derived from general or particular revelation [contrasted] with elegant simplicity of a philosophical argument."[23]

No wonder that calls in Australia for any form of religious argument or opinion to be banished from the public square of this country's secular liberal democracy are becoming increasingly strident. Yet this is a travesty of the neutrality to which a liberal polity ought to aspire.

Liberalism and the recovery of reasonableness

The secular liberal state must aspire to be a neutral state. It must establish, and enforce, principles for regulating disagreements between citizens who adhere to widely diverging conceptions about, for example, what constitutes the good life. Whereas these conceptions, themselves, are hardly neutral, the secular state must remain committed to a neutrality that stands, at the very minimum, for respect for the diversity of those conceptions.

This is an understanding of the modern secular state that has been elegantly expressed by Stephen Macedo[24], a political scientist, who has described the state as:

> Associations of more or less reasonable people who agree on some things and disagree on others, whose reasonableness we wish to respect and whose allegiance we hope thereby to engage.[25]

Any religious reasons advanced for backing a public policy will always be unacceptable to some portion of the wider population. Secular liberals often urge restraint upon citizens with religious convictions who wish to contribute to policy discussions. Such restraint implies that religious grounds for reforming policy must be recast in secular terms.

In the view of many secular, liberal critics of religion, this is the only acceptable form in which religious reasons can ever be presented and propounded in discussions of public policy. It is, the argument goes, a mark of responsibility on the part of the religious citizen to exercise a 'doctrine of religious restraint' by not relying solely on religious reasons to advocate for favoured policies.

On justifying the 'doctrine of religious restraint'
One factor behind the call to exercise restraint is a belief that by invoking religious grounds in support of public policy positions, such citizens somehow fail to show respect to their secular peers and thereby threaten to polarise a pluralistic society. Religion, it is feared, "is surely divisive, and, as such, should be avoided by people of good faith and thus by citizens committed to living in harmony with their compatriots."[26]

The doctrine is a moral, rather than a legal, restraint and can be understood, broadly, in two ways. First, it can be understood as covering only public discussion of policies; and, second, it can be understood as extending to include any kind of religious motivation that might influence a religious believer's decisions about policies.

The doctrine of religious restraint does not call for a thoroughgoing privatisation of religious belief which excludes it from any engagement. Kraig Beyerlein, a sociologist, and Christopher Eberle[27], a philosopher, have noted that the doctrine advocated by secular liberals is fundamentally *inclusive* rather than *exclusive*:

> [The position of secular liberals] is not that citizens should refrain from supporting coercive laws for religious reasons, but that citizens should also include secular reasons in their rationale for this support. Citizens are free to have religious reasons, and even to care about them, but they must also have secular reasons for their favoured public policies.[28]

Proponents of the doctrine accept that religious convictions can form part of the reason a citizen may advocate a coercive law; they simply cannot be the *only* component. Where religious convictions cannot be complemented by secular ones, they must be privatised.

But as Beyerlein and Eberle note, if a citizen has a compelling religious rationale for supporting a public policy, why should those convictions be excluded? "Surely the strong presumption should be that citizens may make political decisions in accord with the dictates of conscience, *irrespective* of whether the dictates of conscience arise from religious or secular considerations." [Italics in original][29]

If citizens *are* committed to living in harmony and to engaging critically in discussions of public policy, it is hard to understand why sincerely expressed views based on religious grounds should be considered disrespectful. As Beyerlein and Eberle have remarked:

> Religious reasons are no more and no less controversial

than secular reasons and so it is arbitrary to appeal to
divisiveness as a basis for advocating restraint regarding
religious reasons but *not* secular ones.[30] [Italics in original]

Appeals to the doctrine of restraint represent an attempt
to limit the contribution that religion can make to public
policy discussion. They are made on the assumption, first,
that whatever contribution religion might make to such
discussion, it will be an unhelpful one; and, second, that
secular reasons are, therefore, always to be preferred to
religious ones.

Yet, as noted earlier, religion continues to make a
distinctive and important contribution to Australia's liberal,
secular society. This contribution might well serve to
undermine secularist certainty about the inevitable demise
of religion. But other factors are also in play that account for
resurgence of interest in religion.

Religion in a post-secular society

The re-emergence of religion is unlikely to reverse the process
of secularization. At the very least, however, it may challenge
the pace of its progress and change public awareness of
religion. If that is so, the very nature of a secularized society
may have to be reconsidered.

Jürgen Habermas[31] has considered the impact of religion's
resurgence on secular society in some retail. He has queried
the progress of secularisation and used the term, "post-
secular society", to describe a secularized environment
which needs to adjust itself to the continuing existence of
religious communities and the influence they exert.[32]

One factor that Habermas argues helps to explain this
shift in public consciousness is that religious groups are
increasingly functioning in the public sphere as what he
calls, "communities of interpretation."

> They can attain influence on public opinion and will
> formation by making relevant contributions to key issues,
> irrespective of whether their arguments are convincing

or objectionable. Our pluralist societies constitute a responsive sounding board for such interventions because they are increasingly split on value conflicts requiring political regulation.[33]

Whereas proponents of the secularization thesis insist that religion is disappearing from public life in the course of modernization, Habermas's argues that, on the contrary, the influence and relevance of religion continues to grow. On the basis of Habermas' analysis, it seems appropriate to describe Australia not simply as a secular society, but as a *post-secular* one where religion, if not resurgent, is certainly re-emergent.

One challenge confronting a post-secular society, such as Australia, is to ensure that a plurality of cultural and religious world-views does not undermine the civic cohesion of the secular liberal state. How, then, should citizens live in a post-secular society?

Citizenship and the reciprocity of expectations

All citizens share membership of an inclusive community – the democratic state. Life in the post-secular democratic state is, therefore, marked by the need to strike a balance between the experience of shared citizenship and this increasing plurality of religious beliefs and world-views. The principle that allows this post-secular balance to be struck is tolerance.

Frequently confused with 'respect', tolerance is better understood as a civic arrangement, founded upon the rule of law and the democratic will of the people. Tolerance disarms quarrelling parties and secures peaceful coexistence. Nor is tolerance to be confused with indifference: it entails the agreement by some citizens to concede the beliefs and practices of other citizens that they, themselves, reject.

Furthermore, and more importantly, the practice of tolerance demands of all citizens an expectation of what Habermas describes as "an ethics of citizenship" that extends beyond mere obedience to the law. It requires citizens to practice a reciprocity of civic expectation:

> Religious citizens and communities must not only superficially adjust to the constitutional order. They are expected to appropriate the secular legitimation of constitutional principles under the premises of their own faith.[34]

He acknowledges that the process of learning this ethics of citizenship can be painful. It requires that the norms of citizenship are framed in language that all citizens can understand. In effect, this means that if the citizen with religious beliefs wishes to support a policy for *religious* reasons, those reasons must be translated into secular terms so that consensus may be reached.

This seems to assume that if religiously based claims are to be translated into accessible, secular terms whilst retaining their meaning, both religious and secular claims must, presumably, bear a high degree of semantic similarity. Alternatively, it could simply mean, as James Boettcher[35], a philosopher, has argued that:

> Politically relevant religious judgments are sufficiently supported by secular reasons which bear some meaningful resemblance to underlying religious premises, perhaps by addressing the same themes and values.[36]

Boettcher argues that Habermas favours not so much *close similarity* between religious and secular reasons as *resemblance*. He cites Habermas's example of a religious response to the issue of genetic testing and suggests that the notions of inherent dignity and individual autonomy might serve as partial, secular translations of a religious conception of persons as sacred and created by God.[37]

Lines that separate?

Developing an ethics of citizenship along the lines that Habermas suggests supposes that there is an identifiable boundary between the private sphere of religious utterances and the broader public sphere in which the decision-making processes of the state are conducted. It is observance of such a boundary that makes possible the cultivation of reciprocity in civic relationships.

Habermas is emphatic that the liberal virtue of tolerance must be cultivated and practised to ensure that neither the private sphere nor the public is unhealthily predominant. Mutual recognition is constitutive of shared citizenship:

> The democratic state must not pre-emptively reduce the polyphonic complexity of the diverse public voices because it cannot know whether it is not otherwise cutting society off from scarce resources for the generation of meanings and the shaping of identities.[38]

Indeed, as Boettcher contends, the ethics of citizenship in a plural society will be strained if citizens who eschew religion view religion as irrational and incompatible with modern society. Boettcher also holds that "non-religious citizens must remain open to the possibility that religious doctrines are a source of important moral intuitions and judgments, some of which have not yet received an adequate secular translation."[39]

But are plural perspectives, even when translated into secular terms, genuinely reconcilable? If they are not, Habermas's attempt to permit religious citizens to participate in public discussions about policy must fail.

His prescription remains very dependent on being able to define a line of demarcation – Habermas describes the line as a "threshold" – on one side of which religious reasons are inappropriate and, on the other side of which, unrestricted religious argument is permissible. Thus, Patrick Neal[40] remarks:

> If the citizen's claims in the name of a 'pious life' are serious enough to outweigh any claims of restriction on reasons outside the threshold, it is not obvious why they are not serious enough to outweigh claims of restriction within it.[41]

The discreet claims of religious and political authority are bound to be intractable. Therefore, it seems that Habermas is striving for consensus where none is likely to be found. If a citizen believes she has a fundamental duty to obey God, and that that duty takes priority over all others, she will be unable to rest assured "that martyrdom at the hands of the political authority will not be expected of her."[42]

This leaves unresolved the outstanding problem of how effectively to describe and defend an appropriate place for religion in a contemporary, post-secular society. One means of resolving this difficulty might be to ask whether it is even possible to describe such a demarcation in the first place. For as long as secularism is considered to be about the relation between two realms – that of the state and that of religion – keeping them distinct will be difficult.

Fixing on religious diversity in a secular society

A better approach might be to stop thinking of secularism as a political arrangement for attempting to keep religion separate from the state, and to begin with the needs and well-being of the individual citizen.

Charles Taylor[43], a philosopher, warns of a preoccupation with what he calls "the fetishization of institutional arrangements". This reflects the notion of 'the people' as the single entity serving as the source of the sovereignty legitimising the state.

It is certainly true that 'the people' expresses the sense of common purpose underlying the democratic state; but Taylor wonders what, and for whom, this state is actually for. The problem is that this notion of collective identity – founded on principles such as the rule of law, and key cultural and social traditions – can assume an untouchable status threats to which, of any kind, must be thwarted.

Taylor argues that secularism ought, instead, to be concerned with how the democratic state responds to the diversity of all citizens in protecting all citizens whatever their outlook. Once a key political ethic essential to the state has been established – such as the rule of law and the protection of human rights – it can be shared by all citizens regardless of their outlook or belief:

> The point of state neutrality is precisely to avoid favouring or not disfavouring not just religious positions, but any basic position, religious or non-religious. We cannot favour Christianity over Islam, but also religion over against non-belief in religion, or vice versa. [Citizens] can concur on the principles, but differ on the deeper reasons for holding to this [political] ethic. The state must uphold the ethic, but must refrain from favouring any of the deeper reasons.[44]

Australia is a country that is growing steadily more diverse in terms of its cultural, ethnic, social, and religious profile. As it does so, the need to balance freedoms enjoyed by a diverse population against historical identities that might obscure those freedoms becomes increasingly important. In Taylor's view, 'fixation on religion' is symptomatic of this tendency to avoid responding to diversity.

Why is religion considered such a threat, attracting the ire of critics such as Richard Ackland, as noted earlier?[45] Ackland's preoccupation with 'religious voices', it will be recalled, hints at a concern that religion is not merely an irritant but actually poses a deeper threat to the integrity of secular society.

Taylor traces this fixation with religious discourse to the very epistemic distinction between secular and religious language employed by thinkers such as Habermas in their efforts to devise a compact between the two realms. It is also fixation with this distinction that drives efforts to limit the use of religious language. The idea, Taylor writes:

> Seems to be something like this. Secular reason is a language that everyone speaks, and can argue and be convinced in. Religious language operates outside this discourse by introducing extraneous premises which only believers can accept. So let's all talk the common language.[46]

The result is that when religious language comes to the same conclusion as secular reason, it is superfluous; when it comes to a contrary conclusion, it is dangerous. Religion and religious language can, accordingly, be sidelined. It is a view widely held, and assiduously promoted, by critics of religion who point to any number of past conflicts between religion and the state to support their view.

Charles Taylor

The point of state neutrality is precisely to avoid favouring or not disfavouring not just religious positions, but any basic position, religious or non-religious. We cannot favour Christianity over Islam, but also religion over against nonbelief in religion, or vice versa.

Sacred and profane: the betrayal of religion

If the process of secularisation is, indeed, irreversible, efforts to introduce religious reasons to the formation of public policy are likely to be regarded as either superfluous or dangerous for some time to come. Proponents of aggressive secularism, in the pursuit of their own peculiar conception of 'neutrality', may well succeed in banishing religion altogether from the public sphere.

But it is the contention of this essay that exclusion of religion in the name of secularism amounts to a betrayal of the neutrality to which a secular society ought properly to be committed. Instead of attempting to segregate the religious from the secular, an appropriate ethics of citizenship needs to affirm a commitment to respecting and upholding the diversity of all citizens.

An Australian secular society denuded of religion will be an impoverished society because religion continues to shape the outlook and aspirations of many. Attempts to deny the contribution that religion and its institutions make in Australia is to ignore its accomplishments and effects, not only in health and education but in general and long-standing influence on law and public policy.

All this matters, according to Ian Harper[47], "because the interplay of competing views and sentiments within the public arena is the stuff of robust democracy. Without it, as Hayek pointed out, the open society is threatened and liberty itself is compromised."[48]

Religion shapes the lives of many Australians and exerts an important influence on the way they participate in families, communities, and wider society. It thereby makes an essential contribution to our shared public life. Continuing antagonism to religion in the name of secularism can only diminish that public life and, with it, the lives of all Australians.

REFERENCES

1   Francis Fukuyama, *Identity: The Demand for Dignity and the Politics of Resentment* (New York: Picador, 2018), 55.

2   I am grateful to Dr Jeremy Sammut for comments he made on an earlier draft of this essay.

3   The final report of the Royal Commission into Institutional Responses to Child Sexual Abuse (Chairman: Justice Peter McClellan AM) was handed down on 15 December 2017.

4   *The New Shorter Oxford English Dictionary*, 5th Edition (Oxford: Oxford

University Press, 2002).

5   Robert Audi (b. 1941) is an American philosopher and political scientist with a particular interest in the role of religion in politics.

6   Robert Audi, *Religious Commitment and Secular Reason* (New York: Cambridge University Press, 2000), 89.

7   On 15 November 2017, the Australian Bureau of Statistics announced the results of the Australian Marriage Law Postal Survey. A total of 12.7 million (79.5%) of eligible Australians expressed their view, with the majority (61.6%) indicating that the law should be changed to allow same-sex couples to marry. All states and territories recorded a majority 'Yes' response. (Source: https://www.ag.gov.au/marriageequality).

8   "Marriage legislation puts religious freedom in doubt", *The Australian* (8 December 2017).

9   Richard Ackland, "Why extend the church's 'freedom' when it's abused what it already has?" *The Guardian* (14 December 2017).

10 In the 2016 Census, Australians were asked to identify their religion in response to the question, "What is your religion?" with the option of "No Religion" placed at the top of the list of available answers. Whereas the 2011 Census showed that 22 per cent of Australians identified as having no religion, by 2016 the figure had risen to 30 per cent, indicating that more than two thirds of Australians continue to retain some degree of religious allegiance and affiliation.

11 Peter Kurti, *Hallowed Institutions: Religion and the Roots of Liberty and Prosperity*, Occasional Paper 144 (Sydney: Centre for Independent Studies, 2016), 21.

12 See further, Peter Kurti, *In the Pay of the Piper: Governments, Not-for-Profits, and the Burden of Regulation*, Issue Analysis 139 (Sydney: Centre for Independent Studies, 2013), 6.

13 Wendy Williams, "Advancement of Religion as a Charitable Purpose in Question", Pro Bono Australia (15 December 2017).

14 Edward Norman, *Christianity and the World Order* (Oxford: Oxford University Press, 1979), 58.

15 COP22 Interfaith Statement on Climate Change.

16 Media release COP22 Interfaith.

17 COP22 Interfaith Statement on Climate Change, as above.

18 Steve Bruce is Professor of Sociology at the University of Aberdeen, UK. He is a leading proponent of secularization theory.

19 Steve Bruce, *Secularization: In Defence of an Unfashionable Theory* (Oxford: Oxford University Press, 2013), 39.

20 Steve Bruce, as above, 55.

21 Steve Bruce, as above, 220.

22 Steve Bruce, as above, 223.

23 Jeremy Waldron, *God, Locke, and Equality: Christian Foundations in Locke's Political Thought* (Cambridge: Cambridge University Press, 2002), 20. See also, Peter Kurti, *The Tyranny of Tolerance: Threats to Religious Liberty in Australia* (Redland Bay, QLD: Connor Court, 2017), 165 et seq.

24 Stephen Macedo is Professor of Politics at Princeton University.

25 Stephen Macedo, *Liberal Virtues: Citizenship, Virtue, and Community in Liberal Constitutionalism* (Oxford: Clarendon Press, 1990), 38.

26 Kraig Beyerlein is a sociologist at the University of Notre Dame, Indiana. Christopher Eberle is a philosopher at the United States Naval Academy. Kraig Beyerlein and Christopher Eberle, 'Who Violates The Principles of Political Liberalism?: Religion, Restraint, and the Decision to Reject Same-Sex Marriage', *Politics and Religion*, 7 (2014), 240-264, 244.

27 Kraig Beyerlein and Christopher Eberle, as above, 243.

28 Kraig Beyerlein and Christopher Eberle, as above, 243.

29 Kraig Beyerlein and Christopher Eberle, as above, 244.

30 Kraig Beyerlein and Christopher Eberle, as above, 244.

31 Jürgen Habermas is philosopher and sociologist whose most notable work is in critical theory and pragmatism.

32 Jürgen Habermas, 'Notes on a Post-Secular Society', *New Perspectives Quarterly* (September 2008), 17-29.

33 Jürgen Habermas, as above, 20.

34 Jürgen. Habermas, as above, 27.

35 James W. Boettcher is Professor of Philosophy at Saint Joseph's University, Philadelphia.

36 James W. Boettcher, "Habermas, religion, and the ethics of citizenship", *Philosophy & Social Criticism*, 2009, Vol. 35 (1-2), 215-238, 228.

37 James W. Boettcher, as above, 228.

38 Jürgen Habermas, as above, 29.

39 James W. Boettcher, as above, 232.

40 Patrick Neal is Professor of Political Science at the University of Vermont.

41 Patrick Neal, "Habermas, Religion, and Citizenship", *Politics and Religion*, 7 (2014), 318-338, 336.

42 Patrick Neal, as above, 337.

43 Charles Taylor is a philosopher whose notable work includes *A Secular*

Age, published in 2007. Taylor eschews the idea that the focus of secularism needs to be on the relation of the state to religion.

44 Charles Taylor, "The Polysemy of the Secular", *Social Research*, Vol. 76. No. 4, *The Religious-Secular Divide: The US Case* (Winter 2009, 1143-66, 1153.

45 See reference 6, above.

46 Charles Taylor, as above, 1162.

47 Ian Harper is an economist currently based at the Melbourne Business School where he is dean.

48 Ian Harper, "Religion Matters for Faith, Hope and Love" in Gary Johns (ed.), *Really Dangerous Ideas: What Does and Does not Matter* (Ballarat: Connor Court, 2013), 38.

3

A SHY HOPE IN THE MIND
Secularisation and religious economic diversity

The idea that economics is or could be a – or even the – theory of everything as regards human behaviour has enhanced its prestige immensely.[1]

Why religion still matters[2]

Those who oppose any appearance of religion in the Australian public sphere frequently argue that it simply has no part to play in a modern, multicultural, secular, and – without any irony – diverse society.

A recent survey conducted by the Australian Broadcasting Corporation indicated that religious belief is not a dominant determinant of identity, social status, or social activity in Australia. Furthermore, 60 per cent of those surveyed thought religion was a private matter and that believers should keep their religious views to themselves.[3]

Critics mount a variety of arguments to support confinement of religion – particularly Christianity – to the private realm of the home, the family, and the mind. One such argument is that religion is inherently discriminatory.

This conviction about discrimination is currently fuelling a demand by a group of humanist societies, which includes the Rationalist Society of Australia, that the Australian Human Rights Commission review the federally-funded school chaplains program.

Established by the Howard Government in 2006, the chaplains program was continued under both Coalition and Labor governments. Its funding of $247m was renewed in the 2018 budget thereby establishing the program on a permanent basis.[4]

Under the program, those to be appointed as chaplains must be acknowledged through formal ordination, commissioning, and recognition by an accepted religious institution. Meredith Doig, president of the Rationalist Society, now wants the program reviewed because, in her view, its structure and operation are "blatantly discriminatory".[5]

The term, 'chaplain', has an overtly religious connotation but the complaint to which Doig's organisation has given its support argues that the work of a chaplain is entirely non-religious and could be undertaken by non-religious people. It argues that the program's selection criterion amounts "to requiring a person be religious. It excludes non-religious people from working as school chaplains." Advocates of the school chaplains program have dismissed the complaint as being motivated by "anti-religion, anti-God, anti-anything non-secular."[6]

This attempt at confinement amounts to a fundamentally illiberal assault on the foundational right to religious liberty. It seeks to restrict the freedom of individuals to pursue their conception of a 'good life' by ordering their own lives, and the lives of their families and faith communities, according to the tenets of that faith.[7]

The arguments in favour of the confinement of religion are themselves highly contentious. The supposed triumph of secularism remains unproven while the continuing significance of religion in Australian society is readily discernible. It is evident, not least, in the growth of Christian evangelical movements as well as the activities of other faiths.

Understanding religion's continuing significance, in turn, strengthens contemporary calls for more adequate protections for religious liberty which have come under threat in Australia in recent times, particularly both during and since the 2017 national debate about same-sex marriage.

Chief among the contentions of opponents of religion is that neither religion nor religious freedom matter. They mistakenly base this antipathy on what they interpret as a decline in *demand* for religion. They rely mostly on successive census returns to support these claims. Where they detect such decline, these critics claim that demand for religion has withered in a modern, enlightened age in which potential consumers of religion no longer need to derive meaning and purpose from a spiritual realm.

By failing to pay attention to overall levels of *supply* of religion in what scholars have described as the 'religious market' – or the 'religious economy' – critics of religion fail to see how different structures of religious markets serve to stimulate – or stifle – demand and thereby affect levels of religious participation.

Supply-side analysis of religion features prominently in the field of study known as 'the economics of religion'. It employs the same assumptions that inform economic enquiry into facets of life such as the family, education, and marriage.

A key assumption in the economics of religion is that religious consumers make rational, informed choices about how to participate in religion – and in which religion. Similarly, religious producers seek to maximise members or resources. Laurence Iannaccone[8], a leading proponent of the economics of religion, notes:

> The actions of clergy, congregations, and denominations

are thus modelled as rational responses to constraints, opportunities, and technologies. As in other markets, the consumers' freedom to choose constrains the producers of religion. A seller cannot long survive without the steady support of buyers.[9]

A supply-side analysis of the Australian religious market, and the behaviour trends of religious consumers, might show a more vibrant and robust picture, and indicate that religion in Australia is rather more healthy than is perceived by critics such as the Rationalist Society of Australia. Such analysis might therefore underline the importance of extending and securing adequate protections for religious freedom.

Before specifically examining this question, however, it will be helpful to review some of the key ideas in the economics of religion.

Exercising rational choice in the religious economy

While the field of the economics of religion is relatively new, scholars probed the economic dimensions of religion long before the 20th and 21st centuries. In *The Wealth of Nations*, Adam Smith, writing about established religions in general, and the Church of England in particular, observed the lack of zeal shown by its clergy in comparison to the enthusiasm exhibited by teachers of religion who needed to work hard for their subsistence:

> In this respect, the teachers of new religions have always had a considerable advantage in attacking those ancient and established systems of which the clergy, reposing themselves upon their benefices, had neglected to keep up the fervour of the faith and devotion in the great body of the people; and having given themselves up to indolence, were incapable of making vigorous exertion in defence even of their own establishment.[10]

Little attention was paid to Smith's insight until recently, largely because, in Iannaccone's view, religion has long been viewed as an institution in decline. Thus the question of whether competition stimulates or retards religious activity went unaddressed. "Proponents of free enterprise," Iannaccone asserts, "will be pleased to hear that Smith's predictions carry the day."[11]

A key idea in an economic theory of religion is that religion is an object of choice. The freedom of the 'consumer' to make a choice about religion serves to constrain the activities of religious suppliers: "consumers *choose* what religion (if any) they will accept and how extensively they will participate in it." [Italics in original][12]

Iannaccone uses the term, 'religious economy', to describe, as a subsystem within the social system, all the religious activity going on in any society – that is, it includes both the supply of, and demand for, religious services:

> Religious economies are like commercial economies in that
> they consist of a market of current and potential customers,
> a set of firms seeking to serve that market, and the religious
> 'product lines' offered by the various firms.[13]

As such, a religious economy is more than a metaphor: it operates in a way that is parallel to the subsystem of the commercial economy in that it involves the interaction of forces of supply and demand for a valued product.

A second principle of an economic theory of religion is that the greater the extent to which a religious economy is unregulated, and therefore market-driven, the more 'religious' a society is likely to be.

Far from debasing and diminishing religion, competition between suppliers of religious 'products' results in greater efficiency and boosts overall levels of religious 'consumption'– just as in the case of the markets for secular commodities:

> Variations in demand result in the inherent inability of a
> single religious product line to satisfy divergent tastes.
> More specifically, pluralism arises in unregulated markets
> because of the inability of a single religious firm to be at

once worldly and otherworldly, strict and permissive, exclusive and inclusive, expressive and reserved, or (as Adam Smith put it) austere and loose, while market niches will exist with strong preferences on each of these aspects of religion.[14]

When the environment is highly competitive, a supply-side analysis of religion holds that religious 'producers' must consider abandoning inefficient activities and unpopular products in favour of those that have greater appeal and are more profitable.

When confronted with choice, the theory, in broad terms, assumes the religious 'consumer' – within the limits of their information and understanding, and guided by their preferences, and following the dictates of reason – will always attempt to select the most beneficial and rational option.[15] According to Rachel McCleary,[16] a prominent scholar of religion and economics, "economic reasoning implies that anything that raises the cost of religious activities will reduce these activities."[17]

In the Australian religious economy, it would appear that believers are losing out to non-believers. But it is important to resist efforts by secularists who behave like monopolists and use public policy and regulation to restrict the market. They achieve this by means of the ratchet effect of creating new rights, using anti-discrimination laws to enforce them. Any challenge to the operation of this new right is met by secularist claims that bigotry and hatred are being promulgated.[18]

Yet the idea that an individual is truly free to exercise rational choice in selecting a religious faith is open to challenge. In the view of some critics, people are frequently socialised into a particular religious tradition because of the circumstances and social context of their birth. And, in some religious traditions, such as Islam, any attempt to choose an alternative faith amounts to apostasy.

In assessing the health of the Australian religious

economy, therefore, it is important to recognise that while freedom of choice and unrestricted opportunity may be defining features of this country and the United States, they are not, perhaps, features of Bangladesh or Afghanistan.[19] Yet the point remains that Australia has enjoyed a long history of religious freedom since colonial times.

Faith and the Australian religious economy

Religion, and a sense of the sacred, has been a thread woven into the fabric of Australian society from the earliest days of the convict colony established in 1788. Eight convicts amongst those transported to Botany Bay on the First Fleet in 1788 were the first Jews to arrive in the colony, the number growing to eight hundred by the middle of the following century.

From the very first, however, Christianity formed an essential component of the colony's political, legal, and social order. Differences between the religious environment in Australia and that prevailing in England with its Established Church soon emerged.

As early as 1836, privileges enjoyed by the Anglican Church were dropped by Governor Bourke who granted government funding to the Church of England, the Roman Catholics, and the Presbyterians on the same terms. A similar policy was adopted with education. All religious schools received public funding until later in the 19th century when free, compulsory, and secular public schooling led to withdrawal of funding of religious schools. All religious denominations were to be treated the same with special privileges for none.[20]

These policies went beyond a mere toleration of difference and an acceptance that people would live apart. As the historian, John Hirst, observes: "The desire for social peace was not a political doctrine. It was not, as the political scientists would say, an acceptance of pluralism."[21] Recollections of bitterness caused by religious and ethnic differences in the countries from which the colonists came prompted a determination to find ways of forging an enduring social peace. The Australian approach was to forge this peace by protecting the religious freedom of all citizens.

It is this principle that informs section 116 of the Australian Constitution, a very broad provision which prevents the Commonwealth Parliament from imposing a religious qualification for certain kinds of position. Section 116 states:

> The Commonwealth shall not make any law for establishing any religion, or for imposing any religious observance, or for prohibiting the free exercise of any religion, and no religious test shall be required as a qualification for any office or public trust under the Commonwealth.

Section 116 secures freedom for the citizen by constraining the power of Parliament rather than creating a new, enforceable right. It represents the Australian religious compact establishing the acceptance of the diversity of religious belief and practice: freedom for all, favour for none.[22]

Perhaps because the social compact was so effective in allowing a diversity of religious freedom and practice to flourish with social and political conflict – sectarian tensions with Irish Catholics notwithstanding – the religious element in Australian society has been understated and discreet. Gary Bouma[23], a sociologist of religion, has invoked a phrase coined by historian Manning Clark – "a whisper in the mind and a shy hope in the heart" – to describe aptly the nature of Australian religion and spirituality:

> There is a profound shyness – yet a deeply grounded hope – held tenderly in the heart, in the heart of Australia. It is not characteristically Australian to trumpet encounters with the spiritual like some American televangelist. Australians hold the spiritual gently in their hearts, speaking tentatively about it. The spiritual is treated as sacred. What is held protectively in the heart is sacred; the sacred is handled with great

care.[24]

David Hilliard,[25] the historian, adds weight to the argument: religion has seldom been allowed a significant role in accounts of the emergence and formation of Australian culture.[26] Popular conceptions of Australia as a society in which religion is peripheral, at best, have contributed to the perceived loss of religion's social significance.

So, just how bad is it? Since the middle of the 20th century, pundits in a number of Western countries – particularly Canada, New Zealand, and the United Kingdom – have been probing statistics which suggest a steady decline in religious belief and practice amongst the population of those countries.

They point to surveys and census returns that appear to indicate a general drift away from involvement in religious institutions believed to have been the mark of an earlier age. Many Australian analysts, activists, and social commentators have drawn attention to very similar trends here.

This is reflected in successive census returns which have indicated a steady increase in the numbers of those claiming no religious affiliation. In the 2016 census conducted by the Australian Bureau of Statistics, the percentage of Australians reporting "No religion" continued to increase – from 25.3 per cent in 2011, to 30.1 per cent.[27] The verdict from the pundits' analysis is unequivocal: religion in Australia is finished.

The Rationalist Society of Australia, for example, holds that belief and action should be based on reason and evidence alone; answers to questions about human existence are to be found only in the natural world. And then, with a generous squirt of hubris, the Society declares, "We're in favour of science and evidence as opposed to superstition and bigotry!"[28]

Release of the 2016 Australian Bureau of Statistics census returns was accompanied, predictably enough, by calls for an end to all religious privilege – whether in terms of tax advantages for religious foundations or publicly-funded expressions of Christianity at Christmas and Easter – and for a more overt public commitment to a secular Australia.

But responses such as these failed to observe that while the proportion of Christians had declined from 88 per cent fifty years ago to just over 50 per cent, Australia has a number of other significant religious communities. Of those respondents who claim a religious allegiance, 52 per cent identify with Christianity, 2.6 per cent with Islam, and 2.4 per cent with Buddhism. The fastest growing religious group are Sikhs who have grown by 74.1 per cent since 2011.[29]

Religion in Australia: what we know so far about the religious economy

The 2016 census returns show Australia's religious profile to be both more complex and more diverse than religion's antagonists – cheered by the rise in proportion of those declaring "no religion" – might have hoped.[30] Religion is not practised consistently throughout Australia and most research into religion and religious life has been confined to patterns of Christian practice, leadership, spirituality, and worship.

For example, in the early 1990s, a number of Christian agencies began a venture called National Church Life Survey (NCLS) Research. The aim was to provide information to help churches connect with the wider community.[31] NCLS has since been joined by other research organisations, such as McCrindle Research, which have added considerably to an understanding of Australia's religious profile.

Research undertaken in 2017 by McCrindle specifically concerned attitudes to Christianity in Australia, but was no less interesting for that. It found that only 21 per cent of Australians are active in the practice of religion and that 57 per cent are not active at all.[32]

The highest proportion of Australians in that first, "active" category – 24 per cent – live in Western Australia, followed by New South Wales – 22 per cent. The highest proportion in the second, "not active at all" category – 69 per cent – live in South Australia.[33]

When McCrindle surveyed attitudes of non-religious Australians, he found that 49 per cent of them preferred an approach to life that is rational and 'evidence-based' rather than informed by the supernatural. 14 per cent of those surveyed, indeed, believe that religion is a wholly outmoded approach to life.[34]

The report found that almost half of Australians who identify with Christianity – 49 per cent – do not attend church; they are also most likely to be female.[35] Whereas 22 per cent of Australians say they know a lot about the church, and 60 per cent know a moderate amount or a little, 18 per cent of Australians say they know nothing about it at all.

Nearly half of Australians who identify with spirituality or religion – 47 per cent – have been influenced principally by their household upbringing. Only 17 per cent of those who so identify, and who grew up in a religious household, have chosen to change or abandon their religious identity.[36]

It appears that 48 per cent of Australians are strongly committed to their religious views. Even so, McCrindle's research indicates that a surprisingly large number of religious Australians – 52 per cent – would be open to changing their religious views, given the right circumstances and evidence.

Of these, it is members of the younger generations who are most open to making a change: 20 per cent amongst Gen Z, and 19 per cent amongst Gen Y.[37] According to McCrindle, 57 per cent of Australians identifying with Christianity are open to changing their views on religion.[38]

Greater openness to changing religious beliefs is one conspicuous feature of the rapid social change that has occurred in Australian society and churches during the past forty or fifty years. The National Church Life Survey adopts the framework of "belonging, believing, and behaving" to track these shifts in religious affiliation, belief, and participation.[39]

In a review of nine core qualities of church health and vitality, NCLS found there has been an overall decline in all indicators in Protestant churches during the past twenty years.[40] But the signs are not all discouraging:

> One important feature of [the] twenty year review is that the trends are either stable or positive across most of the core qualities of church life. We see a consolidation across Protestant church life. The reality of a changing context has largely been accepted. Attention has turned to sharpening clarity about the core practices related to mission, discipleship, service and worship.[41]

Openness to change of religion, reviving patterns of affiliation, and encouraging signs of engagement with religion suggests that the exchange of ideas between individuals who may or may not believe is of continuing importance. McCrindle, interestingly, found that 31 per cent of Australians are "most prompted to think about spiritual, religious or metaphysical things through conversations with other people." Prompts that are reflective of a life stage differ between generations:

> After conversations with people, social media is most influential for Generation Z (32 per cent), whereas reading a book or article (25 per cent) and personal unhappiness (22 per cent) are next likely to prompt thoughts in Generation Y. A major life crisis is the second greatest prompt for Generation X (21 per cent). Global and national issues (26 per cent) and a death in the family (24 per cent) are more likely to prompt thoughts in Baby Boomers than other generations.[42]

These patterns of exchange between believers and other believers, or between believers and non-believers – whether in the form of conversations, written materials, or posts on social media – presuppose a forum where the free exercise of religion is upheld and protected.

Are the assumptions about Australian secularisation correct?

Census returns, together with research from NCLS and McCrindle, therefore, indicate that whilst the religious profile of Australia is clearly changing, religion in Australia is certainly not dead. Non-belief is certainly not the new normal.[43]

Findings such as these are enough to warrant a measure of circumspection about the process of secularization commonly held to have been underway in Australia since the middle of the 20th century.

In addition, Hilliard has alerted us to two other trends in Australian religious life. First there is emergence of new expressions of religious meaning in response to what he calls "the secularization of public culture", and which happens, for the most part, independently of established religious institutions.[44] Much of this is, admittedly, difficult to quantify and the extent of its impact upon society is, as yet, largely unknown.

The second trend is the change in religion brought about, and revitalized, by the new waves of migrants from Asia, the Middle East, and Africa. For many of these arrivals, religion is a powerful source of identity in a new country. At the same time, Hilliard writes, the growing presence of these religious believers has challenged those Australians who envisage a secular future for the nation:

> Religion is not disappearing from Australian life but it is becoming more diverse, more fragmented and more a matter of individual choice. In the Australia of the twenty-first century there will be a wider range of religious alternatives than ever before but no common story, no shared faith reinforced by social institutions.[45]

The secularists propose a static, binary account of religion in which there are those who believe in 'God' and those who do not. In reality there are many forms of religious belief and many nuanced accounts of 'God'. Far from being static, the Australian religious economy is very dynamic.

The resilience of religion in Australia has been masked, to a great extent, by the vigour with which proponents of the so-called 'secularisation paradigm' have made their case. This thesis, in its broadest terms, holds that as a society modernises, industrialises, and advances in technological competence, the once pervasive religious world-view of an earlier, pre-modern age falls away.

For proponents of secularisation theory, decline in religion is not to be attributed to doctrinal or structural deficiencies – and, therefore, capable of being reversed through reform. As Steve Bruce[46], a leading sociologist and a strong advocate of the secularisation paradigm, claims, "the decline of religion in the West is not an accident but is an unintended consequence of a variety of complex social changes [called] modernisation."[47]

Modernisation affects this social change, Bruce argues, because its processes undermine the power, popularity, and prestige of religious institutions. He also maintains that the 16th century Reformation in Europe played a major part in laying the foundations for liberal democracy:

> What were initially religious arguments inadvertently encouraged individualism, egalitarianism, and diversity, which in turn combined with growing social and structural differentiation to shift governments in the direction of secular liberal democracy.[48]

All paradigms of secularisation hold that modernisation – which includes processes of urbanisation, industrialisation, and technological change – has undercut religion and made supernatural claims more difficult to accept.

Bruce contests the entire exercise of applying economic models to religious patterns of behaviour. Whatever encouragement supply-siders draw from comparing diversity and religious vitality in different places at one time, he argues that it will be overwhelmed by contradictory evidence gained from studying one place over time.

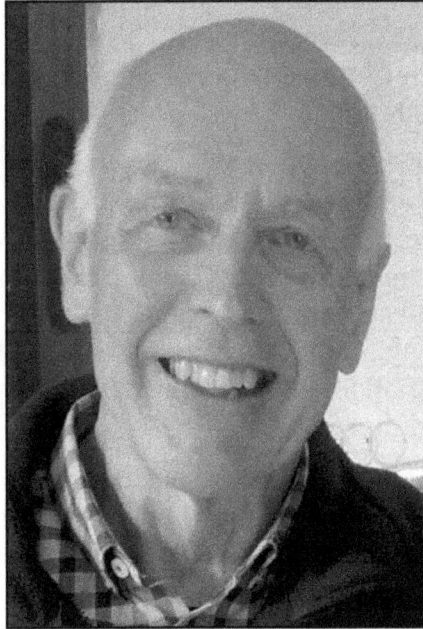

David Hilliard

Religion is not disappearing from Australian life but it is becoming more diverse, more fragmented and more a matter of individual choice. In the Australia of the twenty-first century there will be a wider range of religious alternatives than ever before but no common story, no shared faith reinforced by social institutions.

Religious believers, Bruce maintains, do not behave like consumers in the market place for consumer durable goods:

For most of the world, religion is not a preference; it is an inherited social identity, closely tied to other shared identities. It can only be changed at considerable personal cost. Only in largely secular societies, where there is little religious behaviour left to explain, will people have the attitude to religion supposed by the [religious market] model.[49]

On the basis of empirical observations of such change as increased industrialisation and urbanisation, sociologists developed a theoretical assumption about the marginalisation of religion. Modern societies were considered, for all intents and purposes, to be secular, and assumptions about the irrelevance or meaninglessness of religion sank deeply into the minds of many.

It is beyond the scope of this essay to weigh the specific disagreements among sociologists about what the process of secularization actually entails. What is of concern, however, are the conclusions drawn by proponents of secularisation from empirical observations about social change that occurred during, and as a consequence of, periods of religious reformation and scientific development that began in early modern Europe.

By contrast, Grace Davie[50], a sociologist somewhat critical of the secularisation paradigm, has argued that observed connections between modernization and the loss of the social significance of religion have now become normative – the process of modernisation is held to be *necessarily* damaging to religion:

> With this in mind, it becomes easier to understand why European [commentators] have considerable difficulty accepting the fact that religion is, and remains, a profoundly normal part of the lives of the huge majority of people in the late modern world.[51]

Supply-side analyses of religious markets suggest that these normative assumptions are increasingly open to question. The task now is not to explain the absence or decline of religion, as the thesis attempted to do, but instead to explain and interpret its *presence* in modern societies.

This is especially so when the 'European' way of thinking about religion is applied, for example, to the United States of America – a country were the processes of modernization have not been accompanied by a concomitant fall in religious observance and practice.

In an extensive survey of religious participation in ten Western democracies – which unfortunately did not include Australia or New Zealand – Raphael Franck and Laurence Iannaccone set out to test whether changes in church attendance can be tied to increased secularization.[52] They constructed a retrospective time series which found strong secular trends indicating religious decline in developed Western countries. Yet they could not find any evidence that this decline was actually *caused* by the familiar factors of modernisation:

> Although our regressors comprise most of the variables claimed to undermine religion's plausibility and social significance, none of these variables shows any sign of causing religious decline: neither urbanization, nor education, nor income, nor industrialization, nor fertility.[53]

Although their research did not specifically assess the impact of religious market structure, Franck and Iannaccone clearly doubted that religious decline could be traced either to declining religious competitiveness or to more stringent regulation (for example, immigration controls or planning regulations). "We found much evidence of secularization but no evidence for secularization *theory*. Sacred and secular are woven together too tightly to admit any simple separation."[54] [Italics in original]

American religiosity, together with the rise of Islam as a significant factor in many modern societies, points to new ways of thinking about religion. Theories about religion that emerged in a European context now have limited application in the face of a new set of circumstances, as Grace Davie has noted:

> The very factors that across Europe accounted for the erosion in the historical forms of religion (the negative associations with power and the rationalist alternative) are themselves in decline, liberating spaces hitherto occupied by opponents of certain forms of religion.[55]

Stark[56] and Iannaccone go so far as to propose dispensing

with the term, 'secularization', altogether, and on two grounds: first, because its function is ideological rather than theoretical; and, second, because they find few observable instances to which the term can be applied:

> What is needed is not a theory of the decline or decay of religion, but of religious *change*, providing for rises as well as for declines in the level of religiousness found in societies, and indeed a theory that can account for long periods of stability.[57] [Italics in original]

The term, 'secularization', with which Stark and Iannaccone would like to dispense, is, they maintain, far too narrow. Hence, their encouragement to shift the focus of enquiry away from attitudes of religious *consumers* towards the changing behaviour of religious *firms* – that is, those "social enterprises whose primary purpose is to create, maintain, and supply religion to some set of individuals."[58]

Religious diversity and social policy

Supply-side analysis of religion in Australia is limited and there is, therefore, a gap in our knowledge and understanding of a market-based account of the place that religion occupies in this country. It is a gap that might readily be filled by economists of religion and by the Australian Bureau of Statistics so that detailed regression analyses of religious life can be constructed.

A supply-side analysis, however, is likely to show that far from diminishing in importance, religion has always been – and continues to be – a significant component of Australian society and culture. In addition to augmenting our understanding of religion in Australia, a supply-side analysis can also help to support the case for strengthening protections of religious freedom.

Yet Australians face insistent calls for imposition of restrictions on the open exchange of viewpoints about religion with the purported objectives of promoting diversity, protecting the vulnerable, and eradicating hate speech. These calls, if heeded, clearly pose a grave threat to the fundamental human right to freedom of religion. As Robert Forsyth, an Anglican bishop, has observed:

> Freedom of religion cannot exist in a vacuum, but needs also three other freedoms – of speech, of association, and of conscience – to accompany it. [It] is through speech that religious notions are communicated and contested. It is by being able to associate with fellow adherents that religious community is possible.[59]

Whereas contemporary discussions about diversity in Australia concentrate, for the most part, on race, gender, and sexual orientation, they also need to embrace the religious diversity of our multicultural population. Religious diversity is, in reality, not separate from multiculturalism but a central characteristic of it.

The life of a religious believer is always bound to be, at some level, a public life entailing interaction with, and the organisation of, others. Denials of the continuing significance of religion in Australian society, however contestable, contribute to increasing demand for restrictions to be placed on the free manifestation and expression of religious belief.

This is of special significance because of the questions that religion and religious diversity raise about development and implementation of social policy. Changes to the religious profile that are mapped by census returns mean that no one group dominates national debates about policies in fields such as education, marriage equality, and the provision of social services. In Gary Bouma's words:

> Alliances among religious groups form around particular issues and may not extend to the other issues, making the field much harder for politicians to manage and much less clear for those who implement policy[60]

A more substantial account of Australia's religiously diverse profile provided by a rigorous supply-side analysis would assist development of mechanisms for resolving conflicts that arise from various demands based on different rights such as the rights to freedom from discrimination, freedom of speech, and freedom of religion.

These conflicts already give rise to tension between religious communities and the secular state as the pressure on religious groups to accommodate secular, social norms increases. This has been happening in Australia, for example, with regard to sexuality, race, and gender.

Marked increases in religious diversity reflecting Australia's multicultural society will continue to intensify the complexity of managing social policy.[61] Awareness of this development has prompted undertakings by the Commonwealth Government to investigate the scope of existing protections for religious liberty in Australia.

There is now an acknowledgement that while a culture of religious freedom has thrived, legal protection for religious freedom is limited and there is no explicit protection for religious freedom at the Commonwealth level.

In its submission to the Joint Standing Committee on Foreign Affairs, Defence and Trade's Enquiry into the status of the human right to freedom of religion or belief, the Centre for Independent Studies argued that religious liberty must be upheld as a positive good and not as an exception granted grudgingly by government or Parliament.[62]

In a subsequent submission to the Religious Freedom Review established by Malcolm Turnbull, then Prime Minister, in November 2017 after the same-sex marriage postal survey, and chaired by Philip Ruddock, the Centre for Independent Studies supported a proposal from Freedom4Faith, a religious liberty campaign group, for the Commonwealth Parliament to enact an appropriate federal Religious Freedom Act.

Such an Act would replace the negative protections on which religious liberty currently largely depends with positive protections. It would also complement the tradition of unwritten rights and freedoms protected by custom and common law: "a law which sets out to codify and consolidate traditional [common law] protections could achieve its purpose without creating new rights or limiting existing freedoms."[63]

The sun of religion has not yet set

There are few facets of human society – whether political, social, or economic – that are untouched by the influence of religion. What Grace Davie refers to as "the empirical realities of religion in the twenty-first century" need, therefore, to be reinterpreted and reassessed so that the impact of religion on human society may be appropriately weighed and evaluated.[64]

This essay has argued that a supply-side analysis of religion in Australia would be likely to describe a religious landscape that questions and even contradicts the prevailing orthodoxy promoted by the secularization paradigm.

One of the most important challenges for this exercise of weighing and evaluating is presented by the diversity of the Australian religious economy. Diversity in the religious market entails competition between suppliers; but whereas diversity can stimulate competition, it can also generate conflict.

Hence the importance of ensuring that religious competition in a liberal, secular democracy is framed by prevailing norms and laws. As these broader norms evolve – as they have been doing in Australia with regard to sexual orientation, marriage, and gender – so the pressure on religious groups to accommodate themselves to those norms increases.

In the face of that pressure, and in order to diffuse conflict – as opposed to competition – between differing conceptions of the 'good life', protections for the fundamental human right to religious liberty become even more important.

By testing the relationship between pluralism and participation in the religious market, supply-siders have found a positive correlation suggesting that competition does foster vitality. But this has been questioned repeatedly by critics who level the charge that religious market advocates fail to distinguish adequately between factors of supply and demand.[65]

The battle between religious market advocates and advocates of various forms of the secularization thesis will continue to rage as economists and sociologists on either side of the divide continue to advance arguments and counter-arguments about the merits of a supply-side analysis of religion.

But whatever its flaws – and its limitations and scope do need to be tested further, especially in Australia – one of the principal merits of the religious market model is that it affords an important perspective on the social and cultural place occupied by religion differing significantly from the one that customarily prevails.

A supply-side analysis of religion in Australia will pose new questions and portray a new image of the place of religion in the life of our society and culture.

Whereas the 2016 Census found that some 30 per cent of Australians reported having no religious affiliation – leading to renewed calls for an end to government funding for all faith-based organisations – there remain 70 per cent who do claim a religious affiliation.

And while fewer people may go to church on Sunday, religious organisations are still extensively involved in our society.[66] Many schools, hospitals, nursing homes, and welfare agencies, supplying essential services to all Australians, are religious — specifically Christian. And what drives them is religious conviction. Force them to divorce from their Christian purpose, and those faith-based organisations would quickly fade away and our national life would be the poorer for that.

Despite the secularist protests about the demise of religion and its eclipse by the sun of rationalism, religion is not about to disappear from Australia's liberal, secular society. Multiculturalism, and our intake of migrants, means religious faith will still be with us. And people who believe in God will continue to find themselves in the majority for some years to come.

REFERENCES

1   Jesse Norman, *Adam Smith: What He Thought, and Why it Matters* (London: Penguin, 2019), 188.

2   I am grateful to Professor Ian Harper, Professor Paul Oslington, Dr Renae Barker, Dr Jeremy Sammut, and Simon Cowan for astute criticisms and suggestions as this essay took shape.

3   Annabel Crabb, "What Australians really think about religion", ABC News (6 November 2019).

4   The focus of the program has now been directed specifically to anti-bullying in schools. See, for example, "Budget 2018: school chaplains program made 'permanent'", SBS News (9 May 2018).

5   Paul Karp, "Secular groups call for review of 'blatantly discriminatory' school chaplains program", *The Guardian* (1 April 2018).

6   Paul Karp, as above.

7   For an extended discussion of this issue, see P. Kurti, *The Tyranny of Tolerance: Threats to Religious Liberty in Australia* (Redland Bay, QLD: Connor Court, 2017).

8   Laurence Iannaccone is Professor of Economics at Chapman University in California. He is one of the pioneers of the field of economics of religion which applies economic insights to religion and religious practice.

9   Laurence Iannaccone, "Extremism and the Economics of Religion", *Economic Record* (June 2012), 110-115, 111.

10 Adam Smith, *An Inquiry into the Nature and Causes of the Wealth of Nations* (New York: Modern Library, 1965), quoted in L. R. Iannaccone, "The Consequences of Religious Market Structure: Adam Smith and the Economics of Religion", *Rationality and Society*, Vol. 3, No. 2 (April 1991) 156-177, 157.

11 Laurence Iannaccone, "The Consequences of Religious Market Structure: Adam Smith and the Economics of Religion", *Rationality and Society*, Vol. 3, No. 2 (April 1991) 156-177, 157.

12 Laurence Iannaccone, "The Consequences of Religious Market Structure", as above, 158.

13 Rodney Stark and Laurence Iannaccone, "A Supply-Side Reinterpretation of the 'Secularization' of Europe", *Journal for the Scientific Study of Religion*, Vol. 33, No. 3 (Sept., 1994), 230252, 232.

14 Rodney Stark and Roger Finke, *Acts of Faith: Explaining the Human Side*

of Religion (Berkeley: University of California Press, 2000), 199.

15 Rodney Stark and Roger Finke, as above, 38.

16 Rachel McCleary is an economist based at Harvard University and the Hoover Institution. She edited *The Oxford Handbook of the Economics of Religion* published in 2011.

17 Rachel McCleary, "The Economics of Religion and Secularization", *The Review of Faith and International Affairs,* 5:1 (Spring 2007), 43-47, 44.

18 See Peter Kurti, *Tyranny of Tolerance,* as above, 42.

19 See, for example, Rex Ahdar, "The idea of 'religious markets'", *International Journal of Law in Context,* Vol. 2 No. 1 (2006), 49-65, 59.

20 I am grateful to Jeremy Sammut for directing my attention to these 19th century developments in policy.

21 John Hirst, *Australia's Democracy: A Short History* (Crows Nest, NSW: Allen & Unwin, 2002), 235.

22 For further discussion of the scope of section 116, see Peter Kurti, *The Tyranny of Tolerance*, as above, 142 et seq.

23 Gary Bouma is Professor of Sociology at Monash University in Melbourne. His particular research interests are multiculturalism and religious pluralism.

24 Gary Bouma, *Australian Soul: Religion and Spirituality in the Twenty-First Century* (Melbourne: Cambridge University Press, 2006), 2. Clark coined the phrase to capture what he considered to be the essential character of the ANZAC spirit.

25 David Hilliard is an historian with particular expertise in Australian religious history at Flinders University in South Australia.

26 David Hilliard, "Australia: Towards Secularization and One Step Back", in M. Snape and C.G. Brown (eds), *Secularization in the Christian World* (Farnham, UK: Ashgate, 2010), 75.

27 Australian Bureau of Statistics, "2016 Census: Religion".

28 See The Rationalist Society of Australia (www.rationalist.com.au).

29 There are 125,900 Sikhs in Australia whose numbers grew from being 0.3 per cent of the population in 2011 to 0.5 per cent in 2016.

30 See Gary Bouma, "Census 2016 shows Australia's changing religious profile, with more 'nones' than Catholics", *The Conversation* (27 June 2017). See also, Renae Barker, "Australians have an increasingly complex, yet relatively peaceful, relationship with religion." *The Conversation* (21 December 2016).

31 For more, see www.ncls.org.au. The NCLS is now the most comprehensive religious research venture in Australia, but it confines itself to Christianity. In the following description of religion in Australia, therefore, the terms religion and Christianity are used almost

interchangeably unless more specific use is required by the context.

32 *Faith and Belief in Australia: A national study on religion, spirituality and worldview trends* (Baulkham Hills, NSW: McCrindle Research, 2017). The object of the research was "to explore Australian perceptions and attitudes to Christianity, the Church, and Jesus". The McCrindle report, therefore, has nothing to say about other religions in Australia.

33 *Faith and Belief in Australia*, as above, 16.

34 *Faith and Belief in Australia*, as above, 14.

35 *Faith and Belief in Australia*, as above, 36.

36 *Faith and Belief in Australia*, as above, 15.

37 Generation Y – also known as Gen Y or Millienials – is the demographic cohort widely defined as having been born between 1981 and 1996. Generation Y precedes Generation Z – also known as Gen Z – which is the demographic cohort widely defined as having been born between 1997 and 2012. Generation X – or Gen X – precedes Gen Y and is the demographic cohort widely defined as having been born between 1965 and 1980.

38 *Faith and Belief in Australia*, as above, 17.

39 "Trends in Protestant church vitality over twenty years (1991-2011)", NCLS Occasional Paper 23 (2013), 1.

40 The core qualities surveyed included worship, vision, leadership, innovation, service, inclusion, and faith-sharing.

41 "Trends", as above, 10.

42 *Faith and Belief in Australia*, as above, 19. On the definition of the Generation groups, see reference 36 above.

43 See Peter Kurti, "Not losing our religion", *The Spectator Australia* (3 July 2017).

44 David Hilliard, as above, 86.

45 David Hilliard, as above, 88.

46 Steve Bruce is Professor of Sociology at the University of Aberdeen, UK. He is a leading proponent of secularization theory.

47 Steve Bruce, *Secularization: In Defence of an Unfashionable Theory* (Oxford: Oxford University Press, 2013), 56. Bruce earlier defines religion as "beliefs, actions, and institutions based on the existence of supernatural entities with powers of agency, or impersonal processes possessed of moral purpose that set the conditions of, or intervene in, human affairs." Steve Bruce, as above, 1.

48 Steve Bruce, as above, 39.

49 Steve Bruce, "Secularization", in B.S. Turner (ed.), *The New Blackwell Companion to the Sociology of Religion* (Oxford: Blackwell Publishing, 2010), 137-8.

50 Grace Davie is a sociologist of religion based at the University of Exeter in the United Kingdom.

51 Grace Davie, "Resacralization", in B.S Turned (ed.), *The New Blackwell Companion to the Sociology of Religion* (Oxford: Blackwell Publishing, 2010), 162.

52 Raphael Franck and Laurence Iannaccone, "Religious decline in the 20th century West: testing alternative explanations", *Public Choice* (2014), 159: 385-414.

53 Raphael Franck and Laurence Iannaccone, as above, 404.

54 Raphael Franck and Laurence Iannaccone, as above, 406.

55 Grace Davie, as above, 168.

56 Rodney Stark is a sociologist of religion who is currently Professor of Social Sciences at Baylor University in Texas. He has written extensively about Christianity and comparative religion.

57 Rodney Stark and Laurence Iannaccone, "A Supply-Side Reinterpretation of the 'Secularization' of Europe", *Journal for the Scientific Study of Religion,* Vol. 33, No. 3 (Sept 1994), 230-252, 231.

58 Rodney Stark and Laurence Iannaccone, as above, 232.

59 Robert Forsyth, "Religious Freedom under Challenge?" in Peter Kurti (ed.), *A Quartet of Freedoms: Freedom of Religion, Speech, Association and Conscience* (St Leonards, NSW: The Centre for Independent Studies, 2014), 6.

60 Gary Bouma, "Religious diversity: and social policy: an Australian dilemma", *Australian Journal of Social Issues,* Vol. 47, No., 3 (2012), 281-295, 288.

61 See, for example, Gary Bouma, as above, 293.

62 Submission to the Inquiry into the Status of the Human Right to Freedom of Religion or Belief (Sydney, NSW: Centre for Independent Studies, 22 March 2017), 6.

63 Submission to the Expert Panel on Religious Freedom (Sydney, NSW: Centre for Independent Studies, 7 February 2018), 4.

64 Grace Davie, as above, 175.

65 See, for example, Rex Ahdar, "The idea of 'religious markets'", *International Journal of Law in Context,* Vol. 2 No. 1 (2006), 49-65, 60.

66 A study commissioned by the Australian Charities and Not-for-Profits Commission in 2015 identified 12,253 charities that chose advancement of religion as one of five possible charitable purposes. These included charities that run hospitals, aged care facilities, and education facilities. Curtin University Not-for-Profit Initiative, Australia's Faith-based Charities (2015).

4

REASON, REPENTANCE AND THE INDIVIDUAL

Recovering the religious roots of Western civilization

Freedom is only possible when freedom is itself constrained. Our individualism is most endangered when the customs, institutions, and obligations of community life are eroded.[1]

On defining 'the West'

Any defence of the religious roots of Western civilization must amount to more than mere dogmatic assertion about the place of religion in our society. It must strive to demonstrate that the very existence of that society is built upon religious principles derived, in particular, from Christianity; those roots continue to feed both our culture and our civilization – a conception that can conveniently be described as 'the West'.[2]

'The West' is an elusive concept, and one that has fallen from favour in recent decades. Yet it is one which we are able to grasp almost intuitively, familiar as we are with the freedoms, rights, and protections we enjoy in a secular liberal democracy. For thinkers such as Roger Scruton[3], Western civilization comprises, precisely, "communities held together by a political process, and by the rights and duties of the citizen as defined by that process."[4]

This is a theme developed by the US President Donald

Trump, in Remarks to the People of Poland delivered ahead of the G20 summit in July 2019 when he spoke about the West and the will to survive:

> We value the dignity of every human life, protect the rights of every person, and share the hope of every soul to live in freedom. Those are the priceless ties that bind us together as nations, as allies, and as a civilization. Our freedom, our civilization, and our survival depend on these bonds of culture, history, and memory.[5]

In these remarks, President Trump hints that 'The West', or 'Western civilization', refers to more than an idea. It embraces a community of free nation states, bound by a common set of principles and practices, and by a commitment to preserving a way of life grounded in the rule of law. Or, as the British journalist, Daniel Johnson, has remarked:

> The West is the culmination of aeons of shared endeavour, and the site of collective memories reaching back deep into the origins of human society. Western civilization is the cathedral of historical consciousness, the temple of time past and time future, the destination of a journey that began in the land we still call holy, with Abraham and Moses.[6]

Another critical feature of Western civilization is that this community of nations was formed from a religious belief and a sacred text held in common. It is this religion – Christianity, with its own roots in ancient Judaism – that is woven into the fabric of the West. While the presence of Christianity in the common cultural currency varies from age to age, Western civilization would be changed beyond recognition were the Judeo-Christian inheritance excised altogether.

This does not mean that it would be a realistic or desirable ambition for a Western nation to be a creedal or confessional state; that is, one where the religion of the prince is enforced as the religion of the people. As the process of secularization gathered momentum in 17th century Europe following the Thirty Years War, the driving need was not for a complete break from Christianity but, as Wolfhart Pannenberg[7], a

Protestant theologian, contends, an end to confessional conflict:

> There was an urgently felt need to get beyond the confessional antagonisms and religious warfare that had disrupted the peace of Europe for more than a century. The turn away from Christianity as the basis of public culture was not, at least in the first instance, caused by alienation from the Christian religion, although that turn may have produced alienation in the long run.[8]

As European secular culture evolved, the status of Christianity changed, too. Yet, as Pannenberg argues, our understanding of the very distinction between the realms of the religious and secular has, itself, been shaped by the Christian faith – in particular, by "the Christian awareness that the ultimate reality of the kingdom of God is still future. The social order and public culture that exist short of the final coming of the kingdom are always provisional."[9]

Secularism and autonomy

One remarkable feature of this major diminution of confessional conflict was emergence of a principled distinction and separation between church and state. The claim of a right to enforce belief, whether pressed by the church or the prince, gave way to evolution of a comprehensive conception of rights that describe and defend a sphere of individual autonomy.

The concept of 'secularization' expresses this fundamental principle of the separation of a private realm from the public sphere which affords, in turn, a realm for the exercise of moral choice and moral obligation. An individual's capacity for moral conduct presupposes an area of free choice. Belief that is enforced, after all, is no belief at all.

Larry Siedentop[10] states categorically that "religion thus became a matter for the private sphere" in his remarkable study of the emergence of the individual. "Liberal secularism sought to protect that private sphere by means of constitutional arrangements that would disperse and balance the powers of the state."[11] The kernel of Siedentop's considered exposition is that liberal secularism is the offspring of Christianity, emerging "as the moral intuitions generated by Christianity were turned against an authoritarian model of the church."[12]

That familiarity with Christian teaching and doctrine has almost certainly reached a low point in these early years of the 21st century leaves Christianity's profound influence upon the shape of our conception of the moral life and the good life of the soul untouched. Having grown from Christianity, Western civilization has left behind its belief and its text, in Scruton's view, "to place its trust not in religious certainties but in open discussion, trial and error, and the ubiquitousness of doubt."[13]

But the West cannot remain the West if it becomes indifferent or hostile to this religious heritage. The task before us, therefore, is to recover an understanding of some of the principal ways in which Christianity serves as the very foundation of the secularism that characterises Western civilisation. Three principal roots of this foundation – reason; repentance; and the individual – are the subject of this essay.

Reason

On 12 September 2006, Pope Benedict XVI addressed the University of Regensburg and presented an account of the Christian understanding of the relation between faith and reason.[14] The lecture created a storm of protest because Benedict referred to a 14th century dialogue, about Christianity and Islam, between a Byzantine emperor, Manuel II, and a Muslim intellectual about Christianity and Islam.

During the dialogue, the emperor made some observations about the relationship between religion and violence. He drew a comparison between the two religions and is quoted as remarking that spreading faith through violence is something unreasonable.

Benedict summarised the dialogue thus: "The decisive statement in this argument against violent conversion is this: not to act in accordance with reason is contrary to God's nature."[15] And that was the crux of Benedict's argument: to act against reason is to act against the nature of God.

The address was widely criticised as antagonistic towards Islam and was roundly attacked as being impolitic. The Pope, however, was really addressing his remarks to intellectuals in the West, especially, as Richard John Neuhaus[16], a Roman Catholic commentator, remarked, to theologians and philosophers:

> To theologians who try to pit authentically biblical Christianity against the Greek intellectual inheritance, thus abandoning the great achievement of the Church's synthesis of faith and reason; and to philosophers, Christian and non-Christian, who have accepted a modern understanding of reason that reduces it to what counts as 'science', with the same result of sundering faith and reason.[17]

Indeed, many contemporary secularists do declaim that science has delivered us from religion. They often appeal to the Greek philosophers, who insisted that rationality was the fundamental principle of the universe, and for whom science amounted to the triumph of reason.

But a rational universe had also to be an eternal, unchanging, and perfect universe. Change, therefore, could only be illusory, and sense-data had to be untrustworthy. As Edwin Judge[18] has remarked, the unchanging eternity of the universe had to be rejected before the experimental method could evolve.[19] In Judge's analysis, *Genesis*, not Greece, created modern science. "By downgrading the universe into a temporary artefact, made and run by its creator, devout experimentalists gradually opened it up."[20]

To confine religion to the realm of the non-rational also ignores another essential insight, that it was Christianity's appropriation and synthesis of the Hellenistic philosophical tradition that gave rise to that modern conception of reason from which Western intellectuals have attempted to divorce faith.

Pope Benedict's intention recovered and restated the relationship between faith and reason. For if religion belongs to the realm of the non-rational, the discovery of truth can never be part of reasonable discourse and can be nothing more than a series of subjective assumptions. The danger of such a sundering of faith and reason, Benedict argued, is that it results in a grievously attenuated form of Christianity leading to "the image of a capricious God, who is not even bound to truth and goodness."[21]

This is not to suggest that Benedict is advancing an anthropomorphic conception of God; his purpose was to remind us that, between the Creator God and our created reason, there exists a real analogy which is capable of expression in language.

The importance of Pope Benedict's Regensburg address lies, first, in his restatement of the decisive importance of the synthesis of faith and reason in development of Western civilization; and, second, in his recognition of the need to broaden the concept of reason beyond the limits of the empirically falsifiable:

> In the Western world, it is widely held that only positivistic reason, and the forms of philosophy based on it, are universally valid. Yet the world's profoundly religious cultures see this exclusion of the divine from the universality of reason as an attack on their more profound convictions.[22]

Benedict argued that we must reconsider the scope of reason so that enquiry about the nature and purposes of God is once more brought within its fold. After all, Christian theology entails a formal reasoning about God, and this system of reasoned enquiry into the search for truth became foundational in what we refer to as 'the West'.

As Samuel Gregg[23] has observed, this "emphasis on our

minds' ability to apprehend reality – and not just empirical potentialities and actualities, but also philosophical and religious truths – is woven into the West's very fabric."[24]

It is by application of reason that human beings, created in the image of God, have exercised the capacity both to comprehend and to shape their social reality, to exercise moral judgment, and to facilitate what Gregg describes as "wise intellectual and social habits." These habits include a wariness of superstition, and a desire to avoid error, as well as a concern for just relationships, a suspicion of arbitrary power, and an attachment to liberty. "Reason itself allows us to know that we can transform not just the world around us but also ourselves."[25]

By the exercise of reason, then, we may use our God-given free will to make choices and thereby grow as *reasonable* people. And it is in virtue of being reasonable people that we can build human communities which defend human dignity from the indignity of violent assault, the arbitrary exercise of force, and the subversion of courage and character.

Inherent in this is the notion of human progress and the recognition of error, and this leads to a consideration of the second root of the Christian foundation of the West, *repentance.*

Repentance

Although repentance may seem an odd concept to identify as foundational for Western civilization, it does, in fact, flow very naturally from the foregoing consideration of reason.

Repentance comes from the Greek word, *metanoia*, "a change of mind". It presupposes regret, remorse, contrition, and a changing of one's ways. And yet repentance involves not simply an act of the mind: it involves the will and the emotions. In other words, repentance involves the whole human person.[26]

Yet repentance is founded, principally, on the exercise

of reason, deemed by Christians to be the supreme gift from God whereby our understanding of revelation and the scriptures becomes possible. It also expresses belief in the perfectibility of creation – including human beings. As Judge has remarked:

> Classical ethics was focused upon the practice of the virtues, that is the good qualities we possess, rather than upon our response to others. Virtue is put to the test of morality with its high doctrine of personal answerability.[27]

This capacity to reflect on the past and to make amendment of life helps to orient Christianity towards the future and encourages Christians to anticipate the providential action of God. Repentance, in other words, is the seed of Christian hope.

Edwin Judge

Classical ethics was focused upon the practice of the virtues, that is the good qualities we possess, rather than upon our response to others. Virtue is put to the test of morality with its high doctrine of personal answerability.

Roger Scruton has eloquently described the integral place of repentance in the moral and spiritual architecture of the West. He argues this is one of the "quintessential parts of the Western soul and the Christian inheritance."[28]

Scruton associates repentance – along with its concomitant components of confession and forgiveness – with the notion of sacrifice. For Scruton, sacrifice is one of the indispensable habits in Christian culture because it enables individuals to hold one another to account in those matters where our conduct can harm others:

> Those who confess, sacrifice their pride, while those who forgive, sacrifice their resentment, renouncing thereby something that had been dear to their hearts. Confession and forgiveness are the habits that made our civilization possible.[29]

Scruton, talking principally about Christian conceptions of repentance, is right to acknowledge, in addition, the themes of repentance and amendment of life that occur in Judaism, and he cites the rituals and liturgy of Yom Kippur as a notable example.

These rituals are grounded ultimately in the Decalogue, the immutable, rational, and consistent moral code that remains one of the most significant components of the Judaic legacy undergirding the West and its life. Judaism, Jonathan Sacks[30] has written, "is God's call to human responsibility, to create a world that is a worthy home for His presence."[31]

Repentance, as the liturgical expression of our accountability to God and to one another, is a principal element of Judeo-Christian culture. It is, moreover, a principal tenet of Christian theology that sin is a personal matter: sin inheres in the human heart of the individual rather than in the collective identity of the group. In the words of Rodney Stark[32], a sociologist of religion, "Christianity was founded on the doctrine that humans have been given the capacity and, hence, the responsibility to determine their own actions."[33]

This led, as a consequence to a much wider acceptance of accountability as a feature of public, social, and political life – something that, as Scruton underlines, is completely absent from totalitarian regimes. Democratic elections give electors the opportunity to decide who they will have to govern them; and candidates seeking election to office have, in turn, an appropriate sense of being accountable to the electorate.

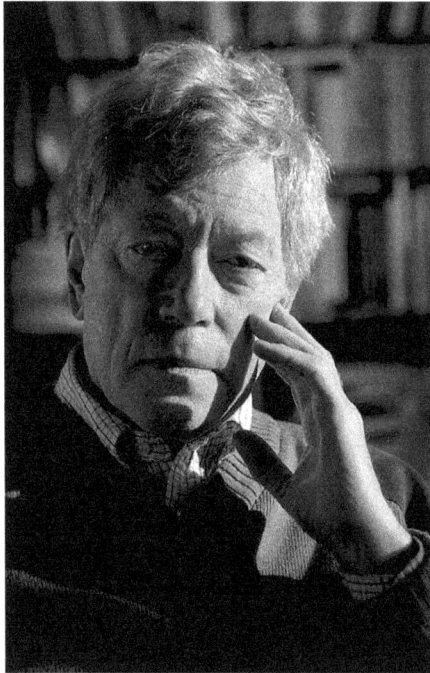

Roger Scruton

Those who confess, sacrifice their pride, while those who forgive, sacrifice their resentment, renouncing thereby something that had been dear to their hearts. Confession and forgiveness are the habits that made our civilization possible.

Such consciousness of vulnerability to popular mood is exemplified by our national obsession with opinion polls whereby politicians and party leaders are reminded, with morbid frequency, about their accountability to us and have impressed upon them the need to do better. A belief in the capacity of the individual *to do better*, to change and improve, is a mark of the impact of Christianity on Western civilization.

Stark, himself, draws a distinction between *orthoprax* religions, such as Islam, that are concerned with correct practice and application, and religions that are *orthodox*, such as Christianity, which are concerned with the intellectual structuring of creeds and theologies. The distinction, argues Stark, is, broadly, one between construction and enquiry:

> Legal interpretation rests on precedent and therefore is anchored in the past, while efforts to better understand the nature of God assume the possibility of *progress*. And it is the assumption of progress that may be the most critical difference between Christianity and all other religions.[34]

Progress, and an orientation to the future, have their roots in the exercise of human reason, and are two of the key contributions of Christianity to the foundation of the West.

Others, such as Joel Mokyr[35], an economic historian, argue that Stark has placed too much reliance on an appeal to the affinity between Christianity and reason. Mokyr is critical of what he considers to be Stark's simplistic 'correlation is causation' methodology. It fails, in his view, to establish how one can be the basis of an assertion about the other:

> I know of no metric of reasonableness of religions, though the work of medieval scholasticism obviously tried to place Christian theology on a sound philosophical basis. The notion that there was a direct path leading from Aquinas to modern science and from there to economic development seems speculative.[36]

While the work of Aquinas is certainly an important part of Christianity, Mokyr points out that mysticism and occultism also remained a part. Mokyr argues that by focusing solely on reason, Stark presents "a lopsided view of the intellectual roots of Western civilization."[37]

In making that argument, however, it is important to distinguish between the theological and philosophical principles of Christianity itself, and the institutions of the Church which interpreted and applied those principles so as to protect, strengthen, and wield its power.

The Church certainly has a formidable reputation in pursuing and exercising power with some force by determinedly resisting ideas that did not accord with doctrine. It is this pattern of behaviour that prompts Mokyr to remark that "the success of Europe is largely explained by the failure of Christians to suppress people with new ideas, though not for lack of trying."[38]

Mokyr acknowledges that Stark's provocative contribution is welcome to the extent that it attempts to correct the frequent slights Christianity endures in accounts of the emergence of the West. Even so, he suspects that, in the end, "much like Christianity itself, it is a product of faith rather than of reason or fact."[39]

Mokyr does have a point. Yet even while conceding that, at times – perhaps at many times – in its history, the Christian Church has been extremely intolerant of new ideas, the moral and intellectual architecture of Christianity, as a *system of belief*, fostered human progress. Nor should it be imagined that this system of belief floats freely in some pure realm independent of the Church. Christians only emerge by being formed and shaped as individuals by the Church, or *ecclesia*. Christian practice is always communally embodied in the life of the Church.[40]

Even if a very bleak view of the Church's legacy is accepted, it remains the case that the European environment was conducive to intellectual flourishing in the early modern period. It was an environment that allowed innovation and enquiry to take place and to shape the social and economic life of Western societies.

As such, it is, surely, quite justifiable to argue that it was Christianity – not specifically the conduct of the churches – with its directional conception of both social and human progress, which shaped significantly the environment that enabled all this to occur. At the heart of this progress, a third root of the Christian foundation of the West, and quite possibly the most important, can be identified.

The individual

The Christian conception of the individual is so important because it underlies all the propositions about rights, responsibilities, and liberties that inform Western conceptions of civil society. As Stark has remarked:

> Of the major world faiths, only Christianity has devoted serious and sustained attention to human rights, as opposed to human duties. The other great faiths minimize individualism and stress collective obligations. They are cultures of shame, rather than cultures of guilt.[41]

Whereas the ancient, pre-Christian world had at its heart the assumption of natural inequality, Christianity spun a golden thread that came to link key Western liberal ideas of truth, faith, and freedom – that thread being the principle of individual moral agency and the assumption of the inherent *equality* of all human beings.

To Siedentop this golden thread of individual moral agency can be traced right back to the Gospels, to the writings of St Paul and his exposition of 'The Christ' to describe the presence of God in the world, and ultimately to the teachings of Jesus himself which proclaim the supreme moral fact about humans: that we are all created in the image of God – *imago Dei*.

The genius of Christianity is that by investing every individual with the God-given capacity for exercising individual moral agency, human beings are no longer defined by social status. Life 'in Christ' creates what Siedentop calls "a rightful domain for individual conscience and choice."[42]

During the Middle Ages, canon lawyers and philosophers began to work out the elements of rights which were needed to protect the notions of individual identity and agency. A moral claim about the individual was converted into a social status concerning individual identity. As this occurred, so, too, an understanding of rights evolved to protect the free exercise of that identity. This conversion was made possible by development of the notion of equality of souls from which this commitment to individual liberty sprang.

While never side-stepping the Church's shortcomings in upholding the ideal of individual liberty and freedom of conscience, Siedentop makes the bold claim that because of its central egalitarian moral insight about individual liberty, Christianity played such a decisive part in the development of the individual and the place of the individual in society:

> [Christianity] rests on the firm belief that to be human means being a rational and moral agent, a free chooser with responsibility for one's actions. It joins rights with duties to others.[43]

Secularism, then, does not refer to a non-moral, indifference to religion; it assumes a moral equality of individuals whereby an appropriate sphere of human autonomy is described. Within this sphere, religious belief can be freely developed, expressed, and defended. In Siedentop's words: "It provides the gateway to beliefs properly so called, making it possible to distinguish inner conviction from mere external conformity."[44]

The commitment of liberal secularism to individual liberty is widely taken for granted these days by many in our society who are, nonetheless, opposed to any form of religion – and especially Christianity.

The 2016 Census showed a rise to just over 30 per cent in those describing themselves as having "no religion". This led to calls for a final push to displace religion from any involvement in Australian public life. Those making such demands conveniently overlooked that nearly two-thirds of Australians clearly maintain a religious affiliation of one kind or another, and that Christianity remains the majority affiliate religion.

Larry Siedentop

[Christianity] rests on the firm belief that to be human means being a rational and moral agent, a free chooser with responsibility for one's actions. It joins rights with duties to others.

The aggressive, and somewhat hostile, anti-religious secularism of our own age has scrambled the proper relationship between liberty and faith and, in doing so, has also distorted what should be a healthy relationship between secularism and religion. The radical secularists go further: they pursue a civilization that is not simply indifferent to religion, but strictly neutral as to any conceptions of the Good Life that make demands upon us.

Far from being an irreconcilable opponent of religion, secularism ought, by contrast, to be understood as describing the societal environment both in which religious belief can flourish freely – and in which different religious believers can continue to contend freely for followers.[45]

The missionary effect and the roots of the West

The claim that the Judeo-Christian tradition forms an essential foundation of liberal democracy and Western civilization is widely contested these days. Resistance to religion is growing in many Western countries, including Australia.

Yet the immense debt that liberal democracy owes to Christianity has been shown to be more than merely a rhetorical flourish. It has been tested rigorously and substantially by empirical research.

Robert Woodberry[46], a political scientist who has devoted a great deal of time to researching the relationship between democracy and religion, has looked at developing countries to try to answer the question why it is that some countries not only develop over time but develop as democracies. His research is vast and statistically complex. In broad terms, he examines the role of Protestant missionaries and looks at how they shaped the long-term processes of development and democratization in the non-Western world.

The results are quite astonishing: Woodberry found that the greater the number of missionaries per ten thousand local population in 1923, the higher the probability that by now a nation has achieved a stable democracy.

Why did this happen? Woodberry concluded that the 'missionary effect' was not to be explained simply because missionaries taught the Christian faith. The missions contributed to the rise of stable democracies because they also encouraged wide-spread education, publication of newspapers and magazines, and growth of a strong spirit of volunteering – all factors contributing to a healthy civil society.

One of the implications Woodberry draws from his research for politics and governance is that religious liberty matters because it influences economic and political conditions. It matters even, as he says, "if you're not a religious person, or even if you don't like the types of religious people who do mission work." Woodberry concludes that religious liberty seems to help the poor and help spread power within a society through the process of religious competition and because religious groups help to break up monopolies and elite control over resources like education.[47] Christianity has had a profound influence on what we consider to be 'modernity', Woodberry claims:

> [It] had a lot to do with why some societies now have more wealth and power. Not only that, but religious incentives were important. It wasn't just that they were carriers of things developed by others for non-religious reasons; for many outcomes, religious beliefs actually mattered.[48]

Living in covenant

Reason, repentance, and the individual are three of the principal roots of Western civilization. They are, moreover, roots that are set firmly in the rich soil of our Judeo-Christian heritage. But the danger is that as our commitment to that heritage weakens, so, too, does our capacity to defend the roots of the West that sustain our society, our democracy, and, indeed, our civilization.

Indifference to those roots might well pose a significant challenge to the fabric of Australian society. And, in Australia, the problem appears to be more than one of mere indifference.

According to recent polling conducted by the Ipsos Global @dvisor survey which canvassed the views of more than 17,000 people across 23 countries, 63 per cent of Australians think religion does more harm than good. The average from respondents in other countries was around 49 per cent.[49] Whereas 62 per cent of Indians and 45 per cent of Americans thought that religious people make "better citizens", only 25 per cent of Australians thought so.

There can be little doubt that the social and cultural context in which religion is practised in Australia has changed, and continues to do so. It is, therefore, of considerable importance that we recover an understanding of the important part that reason, repentance, and the individual have each played – and continue to play – in shaping the social bonds that are characteristic of Western civilization.

One concept that expresses the nature of these social bonds and that draws upon the idea, central to Judaism and Christianity, that there is a binding and enduring relationship between God and the people of Israel, is the word *covenant*.

A term rich in meaning, 'covenant' is an important way of describing the relationship that endures between people who entrust themselves to one another, and who accept that entrustment in turn. A covenant goes beyond a contract, therefore, because the focus is not on a stipulated series of obligations but on the relationship between people. 'Covenant' stresses mutual faithfulness.[50]

Jonathan Sacks argues that with a renewed appreciation of 'covenant' we will be able to live in ways that allow us both to be more true to ourselves *and* to be better engaged in the public square.

We know full well that the public square in Australia has become very fractious in recent times as opposing voices are pitched against one another with what appears to be an ever-diminishing scope for nuanced, respectful engagement. What, then, does the Judeo-Christian tradition bring to the public square? For Sacks, who has expressed this idea of religion in the public square very eloquently, 'religion in the public square' means:

> Simply religion as a consecration of the bonds that connect us, religion as the redemption of our solitude, religion as loyalty and love, religion as altruism and compassion, religion as covenant and commitment, religion that sustains community and helps reweave the torn fabric of society.[51]

Once grounded, as we need to be, in the roots of reason, repentance, and the individual – the Christian roots of the

West – we can draw upon a renewed understanding of the importance of covenant as a way of expressing how we bear a responsibility towards one another.

"Never was the need for fidelity and firmness more urgent than now," said Winston Churchill addressing the House of Commons in 1939. Firmness and fidelity are needed now, more than ever if the West is to recover from its present weakened state.

The health of Western civilization depends not simply on the strength of its intellectual fortification but also, as Daniel Johnson, a British journalist, has noted, on fashioning "a bold new architecture that can inspire the young to emulate the aspirations of our ancestors."[52]

Rabbi Jonathan Sacks

[Religion in the public square means] simply religion as a consecration of the bonds that connect us, religion as the redemption of our solitude, religion as loyalty and love, religion as altruism and compassion, religion as covenant and commitment, religion that sustains community and helps reweave the torn fabric of society.

Our commitment to the Christian faith and to our Judeo-Christian heritage needs to be renewed, and that we strive to incorporate the legacy of that heritage in this bold new architecture. If we are resolved to strengthen the Western civilization that has given us individual liberty and the rule of law, then surely we can make no better start than to attend immediately to the health of its Christian roots.

REFERENCES

1   Nick Timothy, *Remaking One Nation: The Future of Conservatism* (London: Polity, 2020), 169.

2   My thanks go to Bishop Robert Forsyth and Professor Scott Cowdell who read an earlier draft of this essay and made a number of important suggestions.

3   Sir Roger Scruton (1944-2020) was an English philosopher whose notable books include *The Meaning of Conservatism* (London: Palgrave, 2001) and *The Soul of the World* (New Jersey: Princeton University Press, 2014).

4   Roger Scruton, *The West and The Rest: Globalization and the Terrorist Threat* (London: Continuum, 2002), 16.

5   Donald Trump, Remarks to the People of Poland (Washington DC: The White House, 6 July 2017).

6   Daniel Johnson, "The Fate of the West", *Standpoint* (July/August 2017), 60.

7   Wolfhart Pannenberg (1926-2014) was a German Lutheran theologian who spent much of his career at the University of Munich.

8   Wolfhart Pannenberg, "Christianity and the West: Ambiguous Past, Uncertain Future", *First Things* (December 1994), 18.

9   Wolfhart Pannenberg, as above, 19.

10 Sir Larry Siedentop (b. 1936) is an American-born British political philosopher whose most notable book is *Inventing the Individual: The Origins of Western Liberalism*, published in 2014.

11 Larry Siedentop, *Inventing the Individual: The Origins of Western Liberalism* (Penguin: London, 2014), 334.

12 Larry Siedentop, as above, 332.

13 Roger Scruton, as above, ix.

14 Pope Benedict XVI, "Faith, Reason, and the University: Memories and Reflections" (12 September 2006).

15 Benedict XVI, as above.

16 Richard John Neuhaus (1936-2009), an American, was a Roman Catholic cleric, author, and commentator who founded the leading journal, *First Things*.

17 Richard J. Neuhaus, "The Regensburg Moment", *First Things* (November 2006).

18 Edwin Judge is Emeritus Professor of Ancient History at Macquarie University.

19 Edwin Judge, "The Religion of the Secularists", *Journal of Religious History*, Vol. 38, No. 3 (September 2014), 307-319, 315.

20 Edwin Judge, as above, 315.

21 Benedict XVI, as above.

22 Benedict XVI, as above.

23 Samuel Gregg is Director of Research at the Acton Institute in Michigan, USA.

24 Samuel Gregg, "Reason, Faith, and the Struggle for Western Civilization", *Public Discourse* (14 August 2017).

25 Samuel Gregg, "Reason, Faith, and the Struggle for Western Civilization", as above.

26 See, for example, J.F. Childress, "Repentance", in J. Childress and J. Macquarie (eds.), *A New Dictionary of Christian Ethics* (SCM Press: London, 1986), 534.

27 Edwin Judge, as above, 318.

28 Daniel J. Mahoney, "Defending the West in All its Amplitude: The Liberal Conservative Vision of Roger Scruton", *Perspectives on Political Science* (2016), Vol. 45:4, 281-288, 286.

29 Roger Scruton, *How to be a Conservative* (Bloomsbury: London, 2014), 16.

30 Jonathan Sacks (b. 1948) is a British Orthodox rabbi, theologian, and writer. He was Chief Rabbi of the United Hebrew Congregations of the Commonwealth from 1991 to 2013.

31 Jonathan Sacks, "The Challenge Jewish Repentance", *The Wall Street Journal* (15 September 2017).

32 Rodney Stark, a sociologist of religion, is currently Professor of Social Sciences at Baylor University in Texas. He has written extensively about Christianity and comparative religion.

33 Rodney Stark, *The Victory of Reason: How Christianity led to Freedom, Capitalism, and Western Success* (Random House: New York, 2005), 24.

34 Rodney Stark, as above, 9.

35 Joel Mokyr is an economic historian based at Northwestern University,

Illinois.

36 Joel Mokyr, "Christianity and the Rise of the West: Rodney Stark and the Defeat of Reason", *Historically Speaking,* Vol. 7, No. 4 (March/April 2006), 12-14, 12.

37 Joel Mokyr, as above, 13.

38 Joel Mokyr, as above, 13.

39 Joel Mokyr, as above, 14.

40 I am grateful to Professor Scott Cowdell for emphasising this important point.

41 Rodney Stark, as above, 31.

42 Larry Siedentop, as above, 305.

43 Larry Siedentop, as above, 361.

44 Larry Siedentop, as above, 361.

45 Larry Siedentop, as above, 360.

46 Robert D. Woodberry is director of the Project on Religion and Economic Change at Baylor University, Texas.

47 Robert D. Woodberry, *Religion and the Roots of Liberal Democracy*, as above.

48 Robert D. Woodberry, *Religion and the Roots of Liberal Democracy* (The Centre for Independent Studies: St Leonards NSW, 2015). See also, R.D. Woodberry, "The Missionary Roots of Liberal Democracy", *American Political Science Review,* 106: 1-30.

49 Matt Wade, "Ipsos global poll: Two in three Australians think religion does more harm than good in the world", *Sydney Morning Herald* (12 October 2017).

50 See, for example, Joseph L. Allen, "Covenant", in James Childress and John Macquarie, *A New Dictionary of Christian Ethics* (SCM Press: London, 1986), 136.

51 Jonathan Sacks, "Cultural Climate Change", *Standpoint* (September 2017), 51.

52 Daniel Johnson, "We need Churchill's vision of liberty more than ever", *Standpoint* (September 2017), 19.

5

'DYING WITH DIGNITY'

Civil society and the myth of the right to die

The days that have been given us are for learning, for hoping, for growing, for waiting, for turning towards the good even in the depths of sorrow, for lifting up the heart in expectation and in love.[1]

'Dying with dignity' and the yearning for autonomy

The phrase, 'dying with dignity', falls easily enough these days from the lips of many people in liberal democracies including Australia. It is a coded phrase. It refers to the idea that each of us should be entitled to decide exactly how and when we die – as if an unexpected death, or one that comes as a result of illness and not of our own volition, is by that very fact lacking in dignity.

And you do not even need to be terminally ill to decide it is time to go. 'Dying with dignity' is almost being promoted as little more than a lifestyle choice. "The state should no more intrude on personal decisions at the close of life than at any point during it," *The Economist* argued, mourning what it saw as an opportunity to reform the law on assisted suicide missed by the UK Parliament in September 2015. "Governments everywhere should recognise that, just as life belongs to the individual, so should its end."[2]

Proponents of the right to die defend this ownership of the 'end' and argue that they want to uphold the key principle of individual freedom. Freedom is a basic good, they say, and any prohibition is an unwarranted restriction on an individual's freedom to choose how — and for how long — they wish to live. Yet this absolutist view of autonomy comes very close to asserting that the desire or the choice — or even the need — to die must be understood as a *right* to die. Choice is paramount; but choice has little to do with 'rights'. While I can certainly *choose* to end my life and may *desire* to do so, the idea that I have a *right* to do so is erroneous.

By harming the web of social relations and obligations comprising community and family life, claiming a 'right to die' actually threatens to tear at the fabric of civil society and do irreparable harm to the social roles and attachments constitutive of individual identity. Exercising the freedom to end one's own life is coming to be seen as a mark of autonomy and independence of mind. But this view, increasingly widely held, is mistaken because it ignores prevailing social proscriptions about suicide. The 'right to die' is a rhetorical device intended to halt further discussion about the acceptability of self-inflicted death. The 'right to die', in other words, is a myth.

Declaring the freedom to do something is very different from declaring that one has a right to do it. Neither a need nor a desire is identical to a right. Each of us is free to choose to do all kinds of things: to commit burglary, to murder, and to drive under the influence of alcohol. The law does not stop us from committing any such acts; it simply stipulates the consequences we will have to bear if we do commit them — and get caught. But when a particular outcome is desired, rights-based language is frequently deployed in an attempt to turn a freedom to choose that outcome into a right that supposedly guarantees an entitlement to the outcome. As Penney Lewis[3] observes, "Transforming an argument into the form of a right increases its palatability and persuasive force."[4]

Exit International and the medicalisation of suicide

Every death by intentional self-harm has a profound impact on others. It is often the case that such a death causes great emotional trauma among the family, friends and community of the deceased. Grief is likely to be compounded by complicated feelings of guilt and even anger about what the deceased has done, particularly so when the suicide is an aggressive act directed at others. Groups such as Exit International, however, are very active in using rights discourse to promote the palatability of killing oneself intentionally — that is, of suicide.

Founded in 1997 by Dr Philip Nitschke,[5] Exit International argues not only for the freedom to choose to end one's life, but for this freedom to be understood in terms of the exercise of a *right* "to determine the time and manner of [one's] passing." Exit also promotes the primacy of choice by maintaining a steady challenge to the idea that the only circumstances in which a person might voluntarily wish to end their own life are those of a grave and terminal illness. According to the website, Exit International has a worldwide membership of around 18,000 people, the average age of whom is 75 years. Most of its members are "the well elderly" but there is a significant minority who are seriously ill.

For Nitschke and his supporters, death needs to be uncoupled from medicine and understood as an expression of individual preference. Never mind what the doctors say, Exit's website declares, the decision to die is best left to the individual concerned: "Exit's aim is to ensure the individual is fully supported by family and friends and has access to the best available information." But the words and phrases used to convey the apparent reasonableness of exercising that choice — "dying with dignity", "euthanasia", and "deliverance" — are all euphemisms intended to break the taboo surrounding suicide.

A taboo is a social custom offering protection from that which society deems to be an inherently harmful practice. Euphemistic phrases about suicide serve to weaken the taboo surrounding suicide by placing some distance between the comforting notion of a decision freely taken and the stark fact that they actually describe the deliberate termination of human life by one's own hand or with the assistance of another.

The term, 'right to die', has an admittedly wide range of meanings that can easily lead to confusion. One meaning concerns refusal of medical treatment. When faced with medical intervention — such as the use of a respirator or a therapy such as kidney dialysis which are intended only to sustain life and alleviate pain and not to cure an illness — any person has a right to refuse treatment, even if to do so may lead to an increased risk of death. Assertion of a right to refuse treatment looks very like the assertion of a 'right to die'. As Margaret Somerville[6], an ethicist, has argued, however, "A right to refuse treatment is based in a right to inviolability — a right not to be touched, including by treatment, without one's informed consent. It is not a right to die or a right to be killed."[7]

Another meaning of euthanasia does concern the demand not only for discontinuation of treatment but for positive assistance in dying by, say, a lethal dose of a drug administered either by a physician or oneself. Although this also looks very like the assertion of a 'right to die', it might also be described as the assertion of a 'right to commit suicide' or a 'right to become dead'. "At most, people have a negative content right to be allowed to die, not any right to positive assistance to achieve that outcome."[8] Perhaps it is more accurate to say a person is *free* to become dead.

Margaret Somerville

A right to refuse treatment is based in a right to inviolability —
a right not to be touched, including by treatment, without one's
informed consent. It is not a right to die or a right to be killed.

Suicide in Australia: a national tragedy

Free or not, suicide is a national tragedy and the leading
— and increasing — cause of premature death in Australia.
Mortality data released by the Australian Bureau of
Statistics in March 2016 showed that the overall suicide
rate increased to 12 suicides per 100,000 people in 2014 (up
from just under 11 per 100,000 in 2013); the highest rate
since 2001. Men account for a little more than 75 per cent of
deaths by suicide. When it comes to overall rates of what
the ABS calls "intentional self-harm deaths", however,
younger age groups of both men and women comprise
a higher proportion of those deaths with the highest rate
(30.2 per cent) in the 20–24 age group.

According to Ian Hickie, National Mental Health
Commissioner, one of the factors accounting for the recent
surge among middle-aged men is that men who were
depressed during adolescence in the 1990s have carried

suicidal ideation — that is, thinking seriously about suicide — into mid-life. ABS statistics show that in the group of males aged 40–44, 18.3 per cent of deaths are attributable to suicide.

Criminal law codes imposed sanctions for suicide and attempted suicide in the past because of its wider impact on society. Suicide was regarded as an offence against humankind because it deprived one's family and community of a member prematurely, and denied them the opportunity to care for the troubled individual. In many places, the law has now changed. Suicide ceased to be a felony in England in 1961. Reform happened earlier in all Australian jurisdictions — much earlier in the case of New South Wales where the *Crimes Act 1900* abolished the offence of suicide. It remains, however, an offence everywhere in Australia, punishable by up to five years in prison, to incite, counsel or assist another to commit suicide or attempt to commit suicide. Another practice illegal in all States (although legal in the Northern Territory for a time in the late 1990s) is euthanasia — the painless killing of a person suffering from an incurable illness.

The literal meaning of 'euthanasia', from its Greek roots, is easy or gentle death. Some argue that doctors already often practice a discreet form of euthanasia by using techniques of palliative care to relieve suffering; but there is a world of difference between an analgesic and a lethal dose of a drug. It is one thing if pain reduction has the unintended effect of shortening life, but quite another if a medicine is administered with the explicit purpose of killing the patient.

Since few would wish a painful or distressing death upon another, however, the etymology of euthanasia is not a great advance in terms of evaluating the morality of euthanasia. And since the administration of compulsory euthanasia (that is, where a person is put to death painlessly but without their consent) clearly amounts to a murder, it is more helpful to consider the practice of voluntary euthanasia — or suicide; that is, where a person of sound mind seeks the termination of their own life.

The *Crimes Act 1900* (NSW) indicates clearly that one of the factors according to which an act causing death can amount to murder is where it has been done with the intent to kill another person. Accordingly, not only would a person counselling another to commit suicide commit a crime, the provision in any circumstances of the means to commit suicide, such as acceding to an individual's voluntary request for administration of a drug to bring about death, could well be construed as an act of murder.

Groups lobbying for legalisation of voluntary euthanasia contend that when a person voluntarily and freely wishes to terminate their own life, the law should permit them either to be supplied with the means to do so, or to be free to authorise a doctor to do so for them. For the time being, however, any involvement with the suicide of another remains a criminal offence everywhere in Australia.

Rights language and the obscuring of duty

Advocates of the so-called 'right to die' are using the language of rights in their effort to win moral and legal acceptance not only for the idea that human life is not inviolable but also for the primacy of rights over other forms of moral discourse. Rights language has such popular and political force, says Penney Lewis, that it often obscures those other forms, particularly arguments about duties — that is, those specific obligations, legal or moral, that are owed to others and flow from one's participation in civil society:

> Arguments which are not in the form of rights, such as those premised on duties, do not truly disappear from the debate, but rather are transformed into rights discourse while their original form remains covert and unrecognized.[9]

The eclipse of duties that are 'other-concerning' by rights that are 'self-concerning' is critically important. When calls for the freedom to be allowed to become dead are couched in the language of rights, they tend to conceptualise a society composed simply of self-interested individuals intent upon severing all social ties and obligations when they see fit. In such a society, no one owes anything to anyone. This is why the assertion of the right to die is what philosopher Roger Scruton[10] describes as a "claim right" in contrast to a "freedom right".[11]

According to Scruton, 'freedom rights', such as the right to free movement and the right to property, allow an individual to establish a sphere of personal sovereignty from which that person can negotiate behaviour in relation to others. A 'freedom right' amounts to a justified demand made against others that they refrain from interfering with the individual. It is observed or respected by non-invasion or non-action thereby enabling us to establish a society in which consensual relations are the norm. Freedom rights do this by defining, for each individual, the sphere of sovereignty from which others are excluded.

Leon Kass

In civil society the natural rights of self-preservation, secured through active but moderate self-assertion, have given way to the non-natural rights of self-creation and self-expression; the new rights have no connection to nature or reason, but appear as the rights of the untrammelled will.

Claim rights, by contrast, are asserted as a *claim* upon a non-specific benefit such as education, health, a standard of living, or even compensation. They are simply demands that someone else do something or give something that the one demanding has an interest in their doing or giving. According to Scruton, assertion of the 'right to die' is the assertion of a 'claim right' because while it is thought to allow the individual to express sovereignty over his or her life, it simply presumes an obligation owed by the state to the individual — but one that is neither negotiated nor reciprocal. It is the individual alone who decides whether or not life is worth living; his or her decision is not to be overridden by any other institution or structure, whether the state, the church, or the family. For those who assert the 'right to die', the conviction that autonomous individuals are quite free to define their own conceptions of the good is warranted by the presumption of human dignity; this, in turn, is intimately connected with self-respect and the paramount status of individual choice: if this is what I want, I am justified in demanding it in virtue of my autonomous status as a human being. As Leon Kass[12] has remarked:

> In civil society the natural rights of self-preservation, secured through active but moderate self-assertion, have given way to the non-natural rights of self-creation and self-expression; the new rights have no connection to nature or reason, but appear as the rights of the untrammelled will.[13]

Society holds out for the inviolability of human life

At the very heart of the concept of human rights is the notion of the inherent worth of the individual: human beings are due a certain minimal respect — which includes the inviolability of human life — simply in virtue of their being human. This is the very inviolability that guarantees abuses such as torture are always objectively and absolutely wrong. Yet, in the words of neuroscientist Neil Scolding[14]:

> The moment the law, or society, accepts that the rule of fundamental respect [for human beings] can be waived in

certain individuals, whether of their choice or otherwise, the principle is lost. Mere anarchy is loosed.[15]

Proponents of a 'right to die' naturally assert the overriding importance of individual autonomy — what Kass sees as being the expression of the "untrammeled will" — and on this basis hold that the principle of the inviolability of human life can be waived. But Scolding warns:

> The most important reason why belief in such a right is wrong-headed lies in a consideration of society. For both as a society, and for the sake of society, we in fact hold that self-determination, and patient choice, are not moral absolutes. In attempting to waive our personal inviolability in some way the harm is not just to ourselves but, far more importantly, to others around us, to society as a whole. The impact of our choices and actions on society has always overridden autonomy in such instances.[16]

The rhetoric of rights deployed to promote the idea of 'dying with dignity' actually entails a grotesque inversion of the very principle of a 'right'. Developed for the protection and preservation of the individual against the demands both of the state and other individuals, the language of rights has now been commandeered to promote the wants and demands of the 'self' that include the desire for self-negation. For thinkers such as Kass, this individuated 'self' finds its ultimate expression in the self-negating assertion of the 'right to die'.

This new rights rhetoric has little to do with the protective function of human rights but is concerned solely with trying to fathom immensely complex moral problems:

> In trying to batter our way through the human condition with the bludgeon of personal rights, we allow ourselves to be deceived about the most fundamental matters, about our unavoidable finitude, and about the sustaining interdependence of our lives.[17]

Kass has wryly suggested that asserting the 'right to die' is simply "the complaint of human pride" against the injustice meted out by nature against human beings ill-fated, as we all are, to die. "The ill-fated demand a right not to be ill-fated," he writes. "Those who want to die, but cannot, claim a right to die."[18]

Threescore years and ten: standing firm against the autonomy absolutists

The span of human life is short, and death is certain. It is up to us to decide how we use the biblically allotted 'threescore years and ten', but we have a limited number of years in which to make something of ourselves and to create lives that express meaning and purpose. Religion at its best, far from being a code of oppressive rules and constraints, is one feature of society that can help us give such shape to our lives by recalling us to an awareness of our interdependence and the importance of community. Rituals around birth and death, together with those marking important stages along the way, all help to express the dignity that encompasses both the span of an entire human life and the intrinsic value of the person both as an individual and as a member of society.

'Rights' involve obligations owed by, and to, individuals. The health of civil society depends on acknowledging the many responsibilities those mutual obligations place upon us. The absolutist claim to autonomy sits uneasily with the basic principles and requirements of civil society, because a deliberate and voluntary act of suicide amounts to a repudiation of those mutual obligations. We bear a general duty to relieve the suffering of others — but not at any such price demanded by the autonomy absolutists. Doctors have dealt with the problem of prolonged suffering by employing the palliative principle of double effect; in effect to hasten death but not directly aiming to do so, only so as to reduce suffering. But, as Anthony Daniels[19] has observed, "Once it becomes a question of rights rather than humanity, there is a kind of creep: why should the dying have all the best deaths? And who better than a person himself to decide whether his suffering is intolerable?"[20]

Claims for the 'right to die' constitute a one-way ratchet effect in asserting the primacy of autonomy. But they need to be resisted because of the impact such autonomous choices are likely to have on the wider society — on the family, on friends, on the local community — in which we live. We must also resist arguments that none of these considerations can ever outweigh the value of individual choice; indeed, it is these considerations that must override assertions of individual autonomy.

The 'right to die' is a rejection of the duties we owe others and of the claims others have upon us. As such, it is a threat to the social and legal norms sustaining civil society because of its moral assault upon the dignity of every human being. The 'right to die' is a dangerous falsehood — a deception — that must be resisted.

REFERENCES

1   John Cottingham, *How to Believe* (London: Bloomsbury, 2015), 143.

2   "One door closes, another opens", *The Economist* (September 19 2015).

3   Penney Lewis, Professor of Law at King's College London, is based at the Centre of Medical Law and Ethics. She is also the UK's Commissioner for Criminal Law.

4   Penney Lewis, "Rights Discourse and Assisted Suicide", *American Journal of Law & Medicine,* Vol. 27 (2001), 45-99, 77.

5   Philip Nitschke (b. 1947) is an Australian humanist, former physician, and founder of Exit International. In 1996, he became the first doctor in the world to administer a legal, voluntary, lethal injection.

6   Margaret Somerville is Professor of Bioethics at the University of Notre Dame Australia and was previously Samuel Gale Professor of Law at McGill University. She is the author of *Death Talk: The Case Against Euthanasia and Physician-Assisted Suicide*, published in 2001.

7   J.D. Boudreau and Margaret Somerville, "Euthanasia is not medical treatment", *British Medical Bulletin* (2013), 106; 45-66, 60.

8   J.D. Boudreau and Margaret Somerville, as above, 60.

9   Penney Lewis, as above, 76.

10 Sir Roger Scruton (1944-2020) was a conservative English philosopher.

11 Roger Scruton, *How To Be a Conservative* (London: Bloomsbury, 2014), 75.

12 Leon R. Kass (b. 1939) is an American physician and bioethicist who is based at the University of Chicago and the American Enterprise Institute.

13 Leon R. Kass, as above, 42.

14 Neil Scolding is Professor of Clinical Neurosciences at the University of Bristol, UK.

15 Neil Scolding, "Right to Die?", *Brain* (2011), 318-321, 320.

16 Neil Scolding, as above, 320.

17 Leon R. Kass, as above, 43.

18 Leon R. Kass, "Is There a Right to Die?", *Hastings Centre Report* (January-February 1993), 37.

19 Anthony Daniels (b. 1949) is a psychiatrist and cultural critic also known by his pen name, Theodore Dalrymple.

20 Anthony Daniels, private correspondence with the author (2 June 2016).

6

DIGNITY

A poor reason to legalise assisted suicide

A hazard built into the very nature of recorded history is over-load of the negative; the disproportionate survival of the bad side – of evil, misery, contention, and harm. In history this is exactly the same as in the daily newspaper.[1]

The legislative journey of assisted suicide in Australia

Until recently, it was an offence everywhere in Australia, punishable by up to five years in prison, to incite, counsel or assist another to commit suicide or to attempt to commit suicide.

The criminal law reflected the social taboo about suicide which held the act to be an offence against humankind: the suicide deprived their family and community of a member prematurely, and denied them the opportunity to care for the troubled individual. It was also regarded as self-murder.

Criminal law codes also reflected Judeo-Christian teaching about the sanctity of human life. According to this teaching, a human being is neither the absolute owner of her life nor its author. Created in the image of God, the life of each human being is "entrusted to us by God that it may begin to find its fulfilment in the loving service of God and our fellow human beings. It is not for us to decide for how long it shall be so used."[2]

The criminal law, therefore, imposed sanctions for suicide and attempted suicide both because of key ethical and religious conceptions of human being, and also because of the wider impact of each act of suicide on society. In many places, the law has now changed and the act of suicide is no longer illegal. An eloquent account of the reasons for this legal development was given by Lord Bingham[3] in a House of Lords judgment:

> Suicide itself (and with it attempted suicide) was decriminalised because recognition of the common law offence was not thought to act as a deterrent, because it cast an unwarranted stigma on innocent members of the suicide's family and because it led to the distasteful result that patients recovering in hospital from a failed suicide attempt were prosecuted, in effect, for their lack of success.[4]

Suicide ceased to be a felony in England in 1961. Reform happened earlier in all Australian jurisdictions — much earlier in the case of New South Wales where the *Crimes Act 1900*, passed at the beginning of the 20th century, abolished the offence of suicide. Assisting suicide, however, was another matter.

The *Crimes Act 1900* (NSW) indicates clearly that one of the factors according to which an action causing the death of another person can amount to murder is where it has been done with the intent to kill that person. Accordingly, not only would a person counselling another to commit suicide commit a crime, the provision in any circumstances of the means to commit suicide, such as acceding to an individual's voluntary request for the administration of a drug to bring about death, could well be construed as an act of murder.

In 2005, the Commonwealth Parliament enacted legislation making it illegal to produce, supply, or possess materials intended to promote the committing of suicide.[5] There have been few prosecutions for assisting another to commit suicide and when a conviction has issued, the decision of the court has often been based on the absence of capacity of the deceased to give full consent.[6]

The movement to decriminalise the offering of assistance to another to commit suicide continues, nevertheless, to gain momentum. In November 2017, the Parliament of Victoria passed the *Voluntary Assisted Dying Act 2017* (Victoria). The statute, which only had effect from mid-2019, allows an individual with a terminal illness to obtain a lethal drug within 10 days of asking to die after having completed a three-stage process involving two independent medical assessments.

In order to qualify, the individual must be over the age of 18, have been resident in the State of Victoria for at least 12 months, and be suffering in a way that "cannot be relieved in a manner the person deems tolerable."[7] The new law was based on the recommendations of an expert panel chaired by a former president of the Australian Medical Association.

A few weeks before the Victorian legislation received Royal Assent, an attempt was made in the NSW Parliament to pass the *Voluntary Assisted Dying Bill 2017*. The bill, drafted by a cross-party working group, contained provisions similar to those in the Victorian bill, failed to pass the Legislative Council by one vote.[8] Attempts to pass similar legislation failed in Tasmania in November 2013, and in South Australia in November 2016. In December 2019, however, the Western Australian Parliament enacted legislation permitting voluntary euthanasia; it became only the second state to do so.

Assisted suicide was legal between 1995 and 1997 in the Northern Territory after its legislature passed the *Rights of the Terminally Ill Act* (NT) which had been prepared by the Country Liberal Government led by Marshall Perron.

The Commonwealth Parliament responded by passing a private member's bill promoted by Kevin Andrews, Liberal member for the seat of Menzies in Victoria, which became the *Euthanasia Laws Act 1997* (Cth). The Act removed the power of any Australian territory to legalise euthanasia.[9] The 1997 Act specifically repealed the Northern Territory Act – but not before four people had received assistance in committing suicide from Philip Nitschke.[10]

In mid-2018, Senator David Leyonhjelm (Liberal Democrat, NSW) proposed a private member's bill – the *Restoring Territory Rights (Assisted Suicide Legislation) Bill 2015* – to restore the territory rights to legislate on assisted suicide set aside in 1997. The bill was subsequently defeated in the Senate in August 2018 but the arguments with which it was presented are noteworthy.

Leyonhjelm's bill recognised territory rights to legislate without specifying the scope of any legislation that might be passed in the Northern Territory or the Australian Capital Territory. In his second reading speech delivered in the Senate on 3 March 2016, however, Leyonhjelm's principal concern was clearly to assert the "fundamental and legal right to choose whether we wish to continue living." But there is a catch:

> The law says we are only permitted to die by our own hand, without assistance. And if we are too weak or incapacitated to end our lives ourselves, we are condemned to suffer until nature takes its course. It is a serious offence for anyone to either help us die, at our instruction, or even to tell us how to do it ourselves.[11]

The argument was cast, as so often, in terms of relief from a supposed experience of unendurable suffering. But the force of Leyonhjelm's reasoning means that once permission to grant assistance is afforded to someone in pain, that permission must be extended *a fortiori* to anyone wishing to exercise their freedom to commit suicide. Leyonhjelm added: "An individual may have good reasons to take his or her own life. But even if they do not, it is still their decision to make."[12]

Additionally, if the principle of individual freedom entitles a sick person in pain to assistance in committing suicide, on what basis can that principle be denied to someone who is not sick and in pain but who wishes to die? An example of a person who falls into this category is David Goodall, a 104-year old academic from Perth who flew to a clinic in Basel in Switzerland in May 2018 where he committed suicide with the assistance of medical staff.

The case was unusual because, while enthusiastic about accepting assistance to end his life, Goodall met none of the requirements normally associated with assisted suicide. Indeed, much of the public support for assisted suicide comes from those who think that no one should have to endure a long and painful death. But Goodall was not suffering from any terminal illness and enjoyed good general health; he was just old and frail, no longer enjoying life, and keen to die.[13]

The terminally ill are usually listed as the first and most obvious candidates for assisted suicide, but the categories of eligibility are very elastic and can easily enough be extended to just about anyone of any age who is tired of life. Amanda Vanstone, a former senator and minister in the Howard Government, writing in support of Leyonhjelm's bill, readily admitted:

> There is no reason that we should refuse to end the suffering of two groups of people. First, those who have a terminal illness and are more worried about the quality of their remaining life than the quantity. Second, those for whom just age has taken its toll and whose consequent frailty leaves them incapable of doing much and who do not want to spend their last months being cared for as one does a baby.[14]

Any future decision by the Commonwealth Parliament to enable the territories to legalise assisted suicide must also surely call into question the need for the $85 million committed by the Turnbull Government in the 2018 Budget to fund suicide prevention programs.[15]

Successful passage of legislation in Victoria and Western Australia has encouraged euthanasia advocacy groups such as Exit International and YourLastRight.com (a national alliance of dying-with-dignity and voluntary euthanasia societies in Australia) to increase the pressure on politicians elsewhere for comparable changes in the law.

Not all calls for change come from secular advocates. There are religious groups that favour assisted suicide. Christians Supporting Choice for Euthanasia, for example, claims that "the overwhelming majority of people of faith support choice for voluntary euthanasia", appealing to a 2007 survey conducted by Newspoll.[16]

Similarly, opposition to the legalisation of assisted suicide in Australia comes from a broad cross-section of the community, some of whom are religious and some not. With passage of a law to permit assisted suicide in Victoria, their efforts will be directed to arguing clearly against pursuit of similar changes in the rest of the country.

The 'dignity' debate

Language is deployed in very elliptical ways in the debate about euthanasia and assisted dying.[17] 'Dying with dignity' is one of the phrases that features prominently. A coded phrase, it refers to the idea that each of us should be entitled to decide exactly how and when we die – as if an unexpected death, or one that comes as a result of illness rather than our own volition, is by that very fact lacking in dignity. And, as in the case of David Goodall, it is not even necessary to be terminally ill to decide it is time to go.

'Dying with dignity' is often promoted as if it is little more than a lifestyle choice. "The state should no more intrude on personal decisions at the close of life than at any point during it," in the opinion of *The Economist*, which mourned what it saw as an opportunity to reform the law on assisted suicide missed by the UK Parliament in September 2015. "Governments everywhere should recognise that, just as life belongs to the individual, so should its end."[18]

Yet the demand that the dignity of the person be respected is at the heart of many arguments propounded by both advocates and opponents of euthanasia and assisted suicide. The *Oxford English Dictionary* gives eight definitions for 'dignity', the first two of which are the most relevant here: "the quality of being worthy or honourable; worthiness, worth, nobleness, excellence"; and "honourable or high estate, position or estimation; honour, degree of estimation, rank."[19]

Worthiness, excellence, and estimation, therefore, are the central notions of 'dignity' which is a term of distinction and therefore not necessarily something to be found or expected in every human being. 'Dignity' is clearly not synonymous with life because a person can live without dignity; but human life is obviously a necessary condition of there being human dignity, for without life there can be no possibility of dignity.

But what can it possibly mean to 'die with dignity'? In their appeals to dignity, those on either side of the debate about assisted suicide claim that their position is the ethically correct one. This seems paradoxical; but, as the bioethicist, Margaret Somerville[20], has noted, the paradox is resolved once we understand that each side uses the term, human 'dignity', differently.

According to Somerville, opponents of assisted suicide regard 'dignity' as an *intrinsic* characteristic that human beings have simply by virtue of being human. It cannot be lost or diminished. A full conception of intrinsic human dignity is grounded in the inherent moral worth of human beings – a worth not diminished by disease or infirmity.

Interestingly, Somerville's interpretation does not completely accord with *OED* definitions of 'dignity' which indicate that 'dignity' refers to worthiness and an honourable standing rather than to an intrinsic characteristic. It is quite possible to live without dignity. Somerville's interpretation is helpful, however, for capturing a conception of the inherent value of human life.

Somerville writes that pro-euthanasia advocates "see dignity as an extrinsic characteristic that can be lost with an individual's loss of autonomy, independence, and control." Providing assistance in suicide, pro-euthanasia advocates argue, is a means of restoring control and, thereby, safeguarding the dignity of the individual.[21]

This conception of what may be considered *social* dignity aligns more closely with the *OED* definition of dignity because it is a status that can be both gained and lost. And yet this extrinsic, or social, conception of human dignity is surely impoverished because it means that dignity, thus understood, is always compromised by any form of disability or dependence. But this cannot be correct: an individual can surely enjoy "the quality of being worthy or honourable" whilst living at the same time with disability or infirmity.

It is clear that the word, 'dignity', is used in very different ways in the debate about assisted suicide, and that some uses stretch the principal accepted meanings.

Some have argued, contrariwise, that a subjective approach to 'dignity' always needs to be adopted when discussing ways of dying: if a person *thinks* dying in a certain way lacks dignity, then it would be undignified for that person to die in this way. Christopher Coope, a moral philosopher, observes that "it is easy to see why this is popular for it seems to by-pass our problems with definitions, and it has an attractive air of autonomy about it."[22]

The compassion argument

Fears about a loss of extrinsic, or social, dignity have, undoubtedly, been fueled, in part, by advances in medical technology that can allow people to live much longer lives than in earlier times. In their arguments for people to be afforded relief from the impact of technology, advocates of assisted suicide frequently appeal to compassion which often forms a very strong component of their case.

There are two elements to the argument from compassion.

Compassion: the terminally ill should be forced to stay alive against their wishes

The first element is that people who are terminally ill should be permitted to die when they choose. This, however, fails to acknowledge the extremely important point that if faced with medical intervention — such as the use of a respirator or a therapy such as kidney dialysis which is intended only to sustain life and alleviate pain rather than cure an illness – any person has the right to refuse treatment, even if to do so may lead to an increased risk of death.

At first glance, the assertion of a right to refuse treatment looks very like assertion of a 'right to die'. This is especially so since proponents of assisted suicide frequently demand not only discontinuation of treatment, but positive assistance in dying by, say, a lethal dose of a drug administered either by a physician or the individual patient.

In Somerville's view, "A right to refuse treatment is based in a right to inviolability — a right not to be touched, including by treatment, without one's informed consent. It is not a right to die or a right to be killed."[23]

The call for discontinuation of treatment looks very like assertion of a 'right to die'; it might also be described as assertion of a 'right to commit suicide' or a 'right to become dead'. "At most, people have a negative content right to be allowed to die, not any right to positive assistance to achieve that outcome."[24] Perhaps it is more accurate to say a person is *free* to become dead.

Proponents of assisted suicide often insist there is no significant difference between deliberately withdrawing essential medical life support and deliberate intervention to bring about death because the outcome is the same. But there is a most significant difference.

Letting a patient die at some point is a practical condition of the successful operation of modern medicine, as Yale Kamisar[25] has observed. The same cannot be said of physician assisted suicide:

To allow a patient to reject unwanted bodily intrusions by a physician is hardly the same thing as granting her a right to determine the time and manner of her death. The distinction between a right to resist invasive medical procedures and the right to [physician-assisted suicide] is a comprehensible one and a line maintained by almost all major Anglo-American medical associations.[26]

Compassion: sparing the vulnerable from 'unbearable pain'

The second element of the argument from compassion is that vulnerable patients experiencing what is usually described as 'unbearable pain' ought to be spared discomfort. Yet available data suggests the experience of unbearable pain does not appear to be a principal reason why people seek assisted suicide.

The *Oregon Death with Dignity Act* (DWDA) Data Summaries record in great detail those who have taken advantage of the Oregon law's permission to end their lives by means of a voluntary self-administered lethal dose of medications. As such, they are a reasonably reliable guide to what motivates people to seek a lethal dose.

According to the 2017 DWDA Data Summary, 218 people in Oregon received prescriptions for lethal medications. As of January 2018, 143 people were reported to have died from ingesting the medication.

Of these, 21 per cent gave inadequate pain control as their reason for seeking assisted suicide; for 37 per cent, it was loss of control of bodily functions; for 55 per cent, it was concern about becoming a burden on others; for 67 per cent, the reason was loss of dignity; and for 87 per cent, it was a loss of the ability to engage in activities that make life enjoyable.[27]

If the figures in the DWDA report are representative of other places where assisted suicide is available, it would appear that relief from intolerable pain is the reason for seeking assistance in only a minority of cases. Anxiety about loss of ability to participate in society and loss of autonomy are by far the more prevalent reasons.

That few people appear to seek a lethal dose because of intolerable pain undermines arguments based on compassion advanced by proponents. Critics such as Kevin Yuill[28] are quite skeptical about the argument from compassion: "Much of what passes for compassion is simply reflected fear on the part of those with little prospect of death in the immediate future. [It] is really self-centred fear for one's own prospects."[29]

Flaws in the argument from compassion arise, in part, because of its debatable close association with the concept of 'dignity' to which proponents of assisted suicide appeal. Notwithstanding the problems identified earlier with her analysis of dignity, Somerville's account is nonetheless helpful because it lays bare the subjective element of the responses individuals make to the prospect of death.

Thus, when people advocating legalisation of assisted suicide appeal to 'dignity', the dignity to which they most frequently seem to refer, and which it is held to be important to retain, does appear to be the *social* dignity of independence and capacity and not the intrinsic *human* dignity that comes simply from the fact of human *being*. This conclusion is supported by successive DWDA Data Summaries.

A dignified death?

If the meaning of 'death with dignity' is entirely subjective, dying without dignity will simply be a felt experience. It will mean that merely for a dying person to *think* they were dying without dignity would mean they actually *were* dying in such a manner.

Concern for addressing the 'felt' experience of lost social dignity by the patient lies behind emergence of a form of psychotherapeutic intervention known as 'dignity therapy' pioneered by Harvey Max Chochinov, a psychiatrist.[30] Dignity therapy seeks to mitigate a loss of social dignity and help patients to understand that ingesting a lethal dose of medication is not the best way to restore that dignity. For opponents of legalized euthanasia and physician-assisted suicide, such as Margaret Somerville, dignity therapy offers their case significant weight:

> [Dignity therapy] identifies the reasons people want euthanasia, explains why many of them change their minds, and describes in personal detail what they and others would have lost if [physician-assisted suicide and euthanasia] were available. Dignity therapy can assist health-care professionals to help patients at the end of their lives who see their circumstances as unbearable and have lost a "why" to re-find one.[31]

The notion of 'dying with dignity' advocated by proponents of euthanasia and physician-assisted suicide reflects a state of *pre-mortem* anxiety and loneliness that can beset the terminally ill; a lethal injection which cuts short life is hardly an appropriate way to address this experience of distress or despair. Dignity therapy, increasingly available as a component of palliative care in Australia, enables the terminally ill to reclaim their identity and sense of social dignity.

Death happens to everyone. While it is certainly true that one can die in undignified circumstances – by execution or torture, for example – such a death can, at the same time, surely be a dignified one if the person confronting death does so with a certain spirit of worthiness, nobility, and honour.

External circumstances do not determine the dignity with which death is met. Indeed, it is difficult to understand how the sort of death that occurs naturally can be either dignified or undignified, as Leon Kass[32] has observed:

> A death with dignity – which may turn out to be something rare or uncommon even under the best circumstances – entails more than the absence of external indignities. Dignity in the face of death cannot be given or conferred from the outside but requires a dignity of soul in the

human being who faces it.[33]

Dignity in the face of death is a possibility for everyone as they die; it is something that depends on the character and bearing of the individual who is dying.

The phrase, 'dying with dignity', as it is deployed by proponents of legalizing assisted suicide, is thereby revealed as meaning precious little. It is used to describe the state that precedes death, not the death itself.

Once the categories of eligibility for assisted suicide and voluntary euthanasia extend beyond terminal illness and the experience of 'unbearable suffering' – as they already have done in the case of David Goodall – the dignity ascribed to the *pre-mortem* state will, soon enough, turn upon the human conditions of vulnerability, weakness, and infirmity.

In the 20th century, we have witnessed the consequences of the profound contempt shown, at times, for the weak and the infirm. Now it is important to affirm that those very human conditions do not become the pretext for arguing that a point can be reached when a life is no longer worth living.

REFERENCES

1   Barbara Tuchman, *A Distant Mirror: The Calamitous 14th Century* (London: Penguin, 1978), xxiv.

2   "Suicide", in J. Macquarie and J. Childress (ed.), *A New Dictionary of Christian Ethics* (London: Westminster Press, 1967, 609.

3   Thomas Bingham (1933-2010) was Lord Chief Justice of England and Wales from 1996 to 2008.

4   *R(Pretty) v Director of Public Prosecutions* [2001] UKHL 61, [2002] 1 AC 800 at [35].

5   *Criminal Code Amendment (Suicide Related Material Offences) Act 2005* (Cth).

6   See for example the decision of the NSW Criminal Court of Appeal in *Justins v Regina* [2010] NSWCCA 242 (28 October 2010).

7   *Voluntary Assisted Dying Act 2017 (Victoria)*. See also, Jean Edwards, "*Euthanasia*: Victoria becomes the first Australian state to legalist voluntary assisted dying", ABC News (29 November 2017).

8   "Euthanasia debate: NSW Parliament rejects bill on voluntary assisted

dying", ABC News (17 November 2017).

9   Section 122 of the Constitution of Australia concerns matters relating to the governance of Australian territories. Section 122 provides that: "The [Commonwealth] Parliament may make laws for the government of any territory surrendered by any State to and accepted by the Commonwealth, or of any territory placed by the Queen under the authority of and accepted by the Commonwealth, or otherwise acquired by the Commonwealth, and may allow the representation of such territory in either House of the Parliament to the extent and on the terms which it thinks fit."

10 Philip Nitschke (b. 1947) is an Australian humanist, former physician, and founder of Exit International. In 1996, he became the first doctor in the world to administer a legal, voluntary, lethal injection. See Michael Cook, "Euthanasia activist Nitschke loses legal battle to practice as a doctor", *National Right to Life News* (14 January 2015).

11 Sen. David Leyonhjelm, Senate Second Reading Speech (3 March 2016).

12 Senator David Leyonhjelm, as above.

13 Charlotte Hamlyn and Briana Shepherd, "David Goodall ends his life at 104 with a final powerful statement on euthanasia", *ABC News* (11 May 2018).

14 Amanda Vanstone, "Can't we just be decent to people at the end of their lives?", *The Sydney Morning Herald* (1 July 2018).

15 "Federal Budget: Suicide Prevention Australia welcomes investment in wellbeing of older Australians", Suicide Prevention Australia (8 May 2018).

16 See, for example, Andrew Dutney, "Christian support for voluntary euthanasia", *Monash Bioethics Review* (April 1997). , Vol. 16, No. 2, 15-22.

17 Although frequently closely associated with each other, the terms assisted suicide and euthanasia must not be used interchangeably. In assisted suicide, the individual kills him or herself with assistance; in euthanasia, the individual is killed by another person. The distinction is important: it does not turn on whether or not the individual who dies or wishes to die has given their full, informed consent; it turns on who does the killing.

18 "One door closes, another opens", *The Economist* (19 September 2015).

19 *Oxford English Dictionary* (online edition).

20 Margaret Somerville is Professor of Bioethics at the University of Notre Dame Australia and was previously Samuel Gale Professor of Law at McGill University. She is the author of *Death Talk: The Case Against Euthanasia and Physician-Assisted Suicide*, published in 2001.

21 Margaret Somerville, *Death Talk: The Case Against Euthanasia and Physician-Assisted Suicide*, 2nd edition (Montreal: McGill-Queen's University Press, 2014), xxviii.

22 Christopher M. Coope, "Death with Dignity", *Hastings Center Report*, Vol. 27, No. 5 (Sept. – Oct., 1997), 37-38, 37.

23 J. Donald Boudreau and Margaret Somerville, "Euthanasia is not medical treatment", *British Medical Bulletin* (2013), 106; 45-66, 60.

24 Boudreau, J.D., and Somerville, M., as above, 60

25 Yale Kamisar, Emeritus Professor of Law at the University of Michigan, is a specialist in constitutional and criminal law.

26 Yale Kamisar, "The reasons so many people support physician-assisted suicide – and why these reasons are not convincing", *Issues in Law and Medicine*, 12.2 (Fall 1996), 113-131.

27 Oregon Death with Dignity Act 2017 Data Summary, (Oregon Health Authority: Public Health Division, 2018).

28 Kevin Yuill, an historian specializing in the intellectual history of the 20th century, is based at the University of Sunderland, UK.

29 Kevin Yuill, *Assisted Suicide: The Liberal, Humanist Case Against Legalization* (Basingstoke, UK: Palgrave Macmillan, 2013), 43. Kindle edition.

30 See H. M. Chochinov, *Dignity Therapy* (Oxford: OUP, 2012).

31 I am grateful to an anonymous referee for drawing Dignity Therapy to my attention, and for referring me to M. Somerville, "Dr Harvey's must-read book unpacks what dignity means", *Catholic Weekly* (8 June 2017).

32 Leon Kass (b. 1939) is an American physician and bioethicist at the University of Chicago and the American Enterprise Institute.

33 Leon R. Kass, "Averting One's Eyes, or Facing the Music?: On Dignity in Death", Hastings Center Studies, Vol. 2, No. 2, *Facing Death* (May 1974), 67-80, 70.

7

TERROR IN THE NAME OF GOD
Confronting acts of religious violence in a liberal society

Fear is accelerating, and we need to try to understand it and to think how best to address it.[1]

When people of faith turn to violence

Five people died and at least 50 were injured late in March 2017 when British-born, 52-year old Khalid Masood drove his car into pedestrians on London's Westminster Bridge before fatally stabbing a police officer outside the Houses of Parliament. Masood himself was then shot dead by armed police. The whole course of events lasted just 82 seconds.

Police initially suspected the attacker had acted in the name of an Islamist terror group but subsequent enquiries failed to establish any link between Masood and IS or al-Qaeda. Islamic State (IS) claimed him as one of their 'soldiers' but Masood, himself, appeared to have a keen interest in jihad and is believed to have carried out his terror attack in the name of militant Islam.[2]

Acts of violence perpetrated in the name of religion have been reported with great prominence in recent times, especially in the opening years of the 21st century, owing to the association — whether suspected or confirmed — that these acts frequently have with Islam. Those who commit acts of violence in the name of religion claim they are morally and theologically justified in doing so.

Governments in countries such as Great Britain and Australia invariably respond to such acts of violence by enacting new, enforceable laws or regulations, tightening security arrangements in public areas, increasing electronic surveillance, and assuring the public that the violent actions are not representative of the religion in whose name the perpetrators claim to have acted. These days, that faith is, more often than not, Islam. None of these responses, however, appears to be effective in stemming subsequent acts of such violence, although police and intelligence work almost certainly foils some attacks.

Scholars of religion continue to weigh whether people who kill or injure others are really doing so in the name of their God, as they claim; or whether they are actors merely identifiable as followers of that God. Thus, the response to the Westminster attacks is reminiscent of the reaction of police, politicians, and commentators to the Lindt Café siege in Sydney in December 2014. Just as Khalid Masood was a Muslim, so was the Lindt Café terrorist, Man Haron Monis. Yet authorities in both those cases have been unable — or unwilling — to decide whether the culprit acted in the name of God, or whether one of the identifying features of the culprit who acted was, simply, that he was a follower of a particular God.

Speaking in the House of Commons after Masood's attack, Theresa May, the then Prime Minister of Britain, said, "It is wrong to describe this as 'Islamic terrorism', it is not 'Islamist terrorism', it is a perversion of a great faith."[3] This sort of response is commonly made by politicians when confronted with acts of violence perpetrated by someone who is Muslim. It depends, however, on an assumption that Islam and Islamism are distinct religious forms. This distinction has frequently been called into question.[4]

Mrs May's reluctance to single out Islam as the religious

motivation for Masood's attack — preferring instead to direct her remarks at 'Islamism' — did, indeed, attract criticism. British columnist Matt Ridley, writing in *The Times*, remarked:

> While I completely accept that the sins of extremists should never be visited on the vast majority of moderate believers, I am increasingly uneasy about how we handle the connection between religion and extremism. Islamist terrorism has become more frequent, but criticism of the faith of Islam, and of religion in general, seems to be becoming less acceptable, as if it were equivalent to racism or blasphemy.[5]

Unease about how to respond to such acts of violence is inflamed by uncertainty as to the place religion occupies — or ought to occupy — in a liberal society, and a consequent difficulty in understanding there could even be a connection between religion and extremism.[6] For example, Rabbi Jonathan Sacks[7] has argued that violence has nothing, as such, to do with religion but has everything to do with issues of identity and life in communities. The social institutions and norms that once were founded upon religion, such as marriage, the family, a shared moral code, and the capacity to defer gratification, have lost their force — and the result is that the shared social virtue of hope has decayed.[8]

Statements that an attack by a Muslim has "nothing to do with Islam", or, in Mrs May's words, is a "perversion" of Islam, indicate that politicians — and indeed, also, police forces, journalists, and even religious leaders — are unwilling, or unable, to understand that religious violence often has theological and ideological roots. They also indicate that those who perpetrate such acts are very serious about the claims they believe their religion makes.

Religious violence is a complex phenomenon and its causes are varied. Failure to take seriously the religious component of such violence is an avoidance of the issue: yet to assume that because many people do not take religion seriously, *no* people take it seriously, is a transparently erroneous.

This essay addresses some of the key questions posed for Western, liberal societies by the commission of violent acts in the name of God. It begins by noting how the ideological neutrality of liberalism, as regards religion, immediately sets up some challenges for dealing with religious violence. Then it will contend that acts of terror designated specifically as 'religious' present a particular challenge for liberal societies because of the ambivalence many such societies have towards religion. In considering how best these societies might approach the problem of religious violence, so as to mitigate the disruptive impact they invariably have on social cohesion and community wellbeing, the essay will conclude by arguing that freedom of religion, together with an open, accessible 'market place' for religious belief and practice, is essential.

Whose truth? Pluralism and meaning in a liberal society

Many people in Australia's secular and pluralist society are, today, comfortably of the view that there are many sources of truth; all of which can coexist more or less peacefully. We believe appeals to reason, tolerance, and other Enlightenment virtues will do the work of allowing us to live together in reasonable disagreement about the sources of value.

Pluralists are happy to live with ambiguity concerning the sources of meaning and value. Holding that there are many sources of value and not just one, pluralism rejects the notion of what philosopher Susan Mendus[9] calls "a providential ordering of the universe."[10] It is a mistake, however, to think this absence of an overarching providential ordering warrants an assumption about a wider societal acceptance of pluralism. This is to miss the very problem presented by religious violence.

For religious believers — and especially those with fundamentalist or, worse, extremist views — for the most part reject pluralism. They say there is only one source of meaning and truth. While most religious believers are law-abiding, there are some fundamentalists and extremists who are violent and prepared to kill in the name of that 'truth'. They have no sympathy for their victims, whom they view as enemies of God; and are ready to sacrifice their own lives as martyrs. Dislodging such deadly ideas from the heads of those kinds of believers is extremely difficult.

Disagreement about questions of meaning and value abounds naturally enough in a secular, liberal state. But the state does not aspire to say anything about such disagreement; a point made forcefully by Sacks:

> The liberal democratic state does not aspire to be the embodiment of the good, the beautiful and the true. It merely seeks to keep the peace between contending factions. It is procedural rather than substantive. It makes no claim to represent the totality of life.[11]

Liberalism is the theory and practice of freedom. When religious violence erupts, liberalism needs to ensure that theory and practice come together to ensure society is able to 'keep the peace'. But the presumption of the liberal state's ideological neutrality is challenged when the issue that confronts its stability has specifically ideological roots.

Does religion sanction violence? A brief survey

Each of the world's five principal religions contends with the issue of religious violence; but even when non-violence is an explicit teaching in those religions, exceptions can be found and used to justify violent action. This section gives a very concise survey of what each of these traditions teaches about violence, and how followers have interpreted those teachings.[12]

Christianity - The teachings of Jesus of Nazareth are frequently interpreted as an uncompromising call to pacifism. The issue of whether — and if so, when — it is justifiable to use violence, has, however, taxed theologians since the era of the Emperor Constantine in the fourth century BCE. Theories about "just war" remain central to

Christian thinking about the moral use of violence. Yet even when employed in pursuit of justice, violence is held by many Christians to be wrong.

Islam - Purity of existence is a central component of Islam. Believers are exhorted to engage in struggle or 'holy war' to defend the faith and this has allowed the word, *jihad*, (meaning 'striving'), to become one of the concepts most familiar to non-Muslims. But Muslim theologians do not agree about the meaning of *jihad*: some argue that it only ever refers to an inner, spiritual struggle; others hold that it has martial implications and can justify militant political acts.

Judaism - Violence is endemic in many early books of the Hebrew Bible. The era of Rabbinic Judaism, by contrast, was largely non-violent, despite some violent clashes with the Romans in the Maccabean Revolt (166-164 BCE) and the revolt at Masada (73 CE). Violence may be justified to defend the faith but is not to be used for purposes of political expediency. Some theologians justify the use of violence for the defence of modern-day Israel and to maintain its security.

Hinduism - Killing in warfare was deemed permissible in the Bhagavad Gita and Hinduism sanctioned violence in order to maintain social order. By contrast, in 20th century Hinduism, religious thinkers such as Mohandas Gandhi held that references to war in the Gita were allegorical references to the eternal conflict between good and evil. Hindu militancy has increasingly been justified as the political might of militant Hindu nationalism has grown in strength.

Sikhism - Literature portrays the 16th century founder of Sikhism, Guru Nanak, as a peaceful figure. Yet the peaceful precepts of Sikhism have been interpreted to allow exceptions used by recent militant activists to justify violent acts. The doctrine of *miri-piri* which expresses the idea that religion is to be victorious in both worldly and spiritual realms is often invoked. The symbol of Sikhism is a double-edged sword.

Buddhism - Non-violence is a core principle of Buddhism expressed in the doctrine of *ahimsa*. Even traditional teaching allows for exceptions to the rule, however, which turn largely on the question of intent. For example, armed response to a threat is not prohibited so long as it is a defensive action. Nationalist ideologies in Buddhist societies has been used to justify the use of violence in pursuit of political struggle.

Justifying religious violence

While all major religions appear to be capable of justifying violence, it is a mistake to assume such justifications necessarily draw upon contemporary socio-political factors — notwithstanding that those factors may certainly inform the way religious believers respond to circumstances. Religious violence remains so difficult for Western, secular liberals to understand because it requires an attempt to explain "not only why bad things happen, but also why bad things happen for reasons purported by their perpetrators to be good."[13]

To that end, the distinction between factors used to *justify* religious violence and those claimed as the *cause* of such acts is significant. Justification is largely based upon specific appeals grounded in the metaphysical and theological premises of the religious tradition.

Philosopher Steve Clarke[14] has identified three broad premises that serve as the means to justify religious violence. According to Clarke, these premises are: appeals to a belief that a state of 'cosmic war' currently persists; appeals to a belief in an after-life; and appeals to sacred principles. All three categories transcend immediate social, economic, and political concerns and, because — crucially — they involve the believer's relationship with God, outweigh those concerns. They appeal "to narratives about the intentions, needs, desires, and other mental states of supernatural agents."[15]

Thus, the justifications for violent action developed in the major religious traditions help to explain how the practice of violence is reconciled, in the minds of some followers, with what the doctrines of those religions have to say about violence and non-violence. Contradictions and differences in emphasis nonetheless remain, making it no less difficult to interpret the theological background to acts of violence committed in the name of religion.

Sacred and secular: a volatile mix?

The juxtaposition of 'religion' and 'violence' in discussions about religious violence frequently jars. Religious belief and practice is conventionally associated with promotion or advancement of peace and human well-being. Yet, as the foregoing brief survey of the five religions has shown, the problem of religious violence is a very old one.

There have always been zealots who are impatient with the slow pace of history and with the social and psychological concessions that have to be made to it. The zealot demands perfection — perfect compliance with a divine law by individuals and societies — now.[16]

In Western societies, the ways religion asserts itself are changing. One significant force in this development is globalisation, which gives greater influence to religious diasporas. This, in turn, has brought a new mix of piety and political struggle — a fusion of sacred and secular objectives — in religious institutions. As political scientist Scott Thomas[17] has noted, where violent action leads to the killing of civilians in order to achieve such religious or political objectives, it can, appropriately, be described as 'terrorism':

> Globalisation has blurred the line between religious organisations involved in advocacy, proselytising, or social welfare — for example, Tablighi Jamaat or Hezbollah — and purely terrorist organizations. It is these kinds of both local and global social networks that allow people to support or facilitate the operations of al Qaeda, Hamas, and other illicit groups across the world.[18]

Whereas the blending of religion and politics is

uncomfortable for many Westerners, Thomas notes social, charitable, political and, even, terrorist networks often overlap in the religious world of the global South.[19]

The terrorist attacks of 9/11 galvanised attention on the relationship, in particular, between Islam and violence. Not only did the attacks conform to a pattern of religious ritual, as Mark Juergensmeyer[20] has noted, the commitment of the perpetrators also "touched religious depths, and their *jihadi* theology was suffused with the images and ideas of their religious history."[21] The determination of many Western, secular politicians and commentators to avoid associating 9/11 with Islam showed how unprepared liberal democracy was either to confront the religious roots of terrorism or to comprehend their depth.

The religious roots of terror

Terrorism motivated by religious belief or conviction is often thought to be a new scourge but, until the 19th century, most terrorism was, in fact, carried out by actors whose objectives were primarily religious — although they were seldom without at least some political or ideological objectives. Indeed, the English terms, 'assassin', 'thug' and 'zealot' derive from ancient and medieval Islamic, Hindu, and Jewish terrorists.

Today, terrorism — a very difficult term to define accurately — is broadly understood to refer to violence directed at civilians in the pursuit of political ends, and therefore a secular phenomenon. As Daniel Philpott[22] has remarked: "By 1968, following the global trajectory of secularisation, all of the world's then eleven known terrorist groups pursued solely secular ends."[23] It can, at times, be difficult to disentangle the religious motive from the political — as is the case in the conflict in Ireland where groups identifiable by religious affiliation nonetheless had clearly described political objectives.

When the *primary* aims and identities of the perpetrators

of violence are specifically religious, it is surely correct to describe them as 'religious terrorists'. And even when their motives are mixed, religious terrorists tend to proclaim religious purposes.[24] Philpott dates re-emergence of religious terrorism from 1980 when two of the world's 64 terrorist groups declared specifically religious objectives. By 2005, he estimates that "36 per cent of known terrorist groups were identifiably religious."[25]

Religious terrorism has become not only more common during the past half century or so; it is now also more deadly than secular terrorism, and Philpott has drawn attention to analysis which demonstrates the centrality of religious belief in influencing religious terrorists. This includes a particular — and, sometimes, peculiar — way of reading and interpreting sacred texts so as to justify the resort to violence.

Common themes in these beliefs include divine sanction for indiscriminate killing; violence as sacramental or divine duty; opposition not only to a regime but to an entire 'corrupted' social order; an apocalyptic vision; and appeals to their own followers as an audience.[26]

The conviction that violence is both morally justified and a necessary expedient underlies, for example, the actions of conservative Christians in the United States and Canada who have launched deadly attacks against abortion providers.

Scott Roeder, convicted in the USA for the murder in 2009 of Dr George Tiller, a doctor who provided abortions late in pregnancy, told the court at his sentencing "that God's judgment would 'sweep over this land like a prairie wind'."[27] Another anti-abortion protester, former pastor Paul Hill, was convicted in 1994 of the murder of Dr John Britton. Before his execution in 2003, Hill said:

> I believe, in the short and long term, more and more people will act on the principles for which I stand. I'm willing and feeling very honoured that they are most likely going to kill me for what I did.[28]

A willingness to give up one's life for the cause being

advocated, whether by execution in the case of the Christian anti-abortion militant, or by being killed in a suicide bombing in the case of those acting in the name of Islam, is a distinctive feature of religious terrorism. As Juergensmeyer has remarked, martyrdom and sacrifice — already important components in the history of many religions — are also highly significant features of religious violence as formal acts of self-renunciation.[29]

When acts of terrorism are committed in the name of religion, it is (as noted earlier) the religious component that is often the most perplexing for citizens of liberal societies. Secular commentators often fail to recognise either the extent to which acts of violence are an intrinsic part of the religious world-view of those who perpetrate them, or the extent to which they are endorsed by what Juergensmeyer and Mona Kanwal Sheikh describe as the "broad communities of support that share their same religious points of view":

> It is tempting to deny that such terrorists as al-Qaeda's Osama bin Laden, Israel's Yigal Amir [who assassinated Israeli prime minister Yitzhak Rabin in 1995], or Norway's Anders Breivik were religious, because they clearly had political reasons for defending what they thought were attacks on their cultural communities. Yet they used the language of religion and religious history to defend their actions, and religious organisations have been their inspiration and support.[30]

The events of 9/11 in New York, of 7/7 in London in 2005, and of March 2017 in London, have brought to the attention of the world the willingness of determined zealots to die in the name of their religious beliefs. Islam has an inextricable political component: one of the objects of which is to establish Islamic law and governance in non-Muslim societies. This development represents a significant, global mobilisation of zealotry at the edges of Islam which has "a problem with violent extremism that is out of all proportion to that of other religions today."[31]

Islamic (or Islamist) extremism is directed against those considered to be apostates. In recent years, a great deal of this violence has targeted Christians who have been killed or injured by Muslim extremists. Two Coptic churches were attacked in Egypt on Palm Sunday in April 2017; in March 2016, a Muslim man in Scotland was stabbed to death by another Muslim for having wished Christians a happy Easter.[32]

It is little wonder that many secular critics of religion have no hesitation in identifying religion as the principal cause of violence in human society — "the most prolific source of violence in our history," according to Sam Harris who thinks that, in addition to its history of violence, religion is inherently violent.[33] But is this criticism warranted?

Is religion inherently violent?

The claim that religion is inherently violent seeks to isolate a specific form of violence allegedly fuelled by theological beliefs; but the claim is overly simplistic. Even so, it has become part of conventional wisdom in Western societies and continues to contribute to the formulation of policies affecting issues such as religious liberty and the public manifestation of belief. But does the claim, persuasive though it may seem, have any substance?

Theologian William Cavanaugh[34] has tested the claim of Sam Harris and other commentators. He accepts that some religions do tend to promote violence under certain conditions; but he argues that any response to the argument that religion is *inherently* violent will depend on the way terms such as 'religion' (and 'secular') are used.

Cavanaugh argues, in the first place, that 'religion' cannot be understood as if it were a form of transcultural and transhistorical feature of human life essentially distinct from the 'secular':

> The idea that there exists a transhistorical human impulse called 'religion' with a singular tendency to promote

154

> fanaticism and violence when combined with public power, is not an empirically demonstrable fact, but is itself an ideological accompaniment to the shifts of power and authority that mark the western transition from medieval to modern.[35]

Cavanaugh argues that to hold that religion is a form of life so easily demarcated from the secular encourages the erroneous view that only by severely restricting its access to public power can religion be tamed. It is an argument used, for example, to justify restriction of government assistance to religion or religious programs. A key component of this ideology is that "violence labelled religious is always reprehensible; violence labelled secular is often necessary and sometimes praiseworthy."[36]

It is to expose this erroneous view that Cavanaugh uses the term, 'myth', to describe the idea — so readily adopted in Western, secular societies — that religion has an inherent tendency to promote violence.

The 'myth' of religious violence

In addressing the proposition that religion is inherently violent, Cavanaugh compares and contrasts two approaches to defining religion. First, he considers *substantivist* definitions, by which he means those definitions that attempt to describe religion in terms of specific beliefs about the nature of reality, the nature of God, or the nature of salvation.

The problem with substantivist definitions, however, is that even if 'religious' can be described as a category distinct from 'secular' by the use of terms such as 'transcendence' or 'providence', this reveals nothing helpful about the meaning of 'religion' itself. As Cavanaugh notes, "excluding systems of belief and practices from the list of world religions becomes arbitrary."[37] Substantivist definitions are able to describe the content of belief systems, but do little to identify the causes of violence said to be provoked by such belief systems.

Cavanaugh then considers *functionalist* definitions of religion. These are accounts of religion based not on the content of a belief system but on the way the system functions in terms of the social and political tasks it performs. They are constructed from empirical observation of people's behaviour, not from catalogues of beliefs.

Functionalists say the conventional taxonomies are not what matter: what is important is to include everything that acts like a religion under the rubric 'religion', whether or not it would have been included by conventional accounts of religion. If it looks like a religion and acts like a religion, the functionalist would say, then it is a religion.[38]

The defect of the functional approach is that it allows for an expansion of the category of 'religion' to the point where it can lose meaning.

If the functionalists are correct, there is a case for saying that secular phenomena such as nationalism or environmentalism are also really to be considered as forms of religion. If so, Cavanaugh argues, "there is no basis for including Islam and Hinduism in the indictment of religious violence while excluding US nationalism and Marxism."[39] The category of 'religion' can become so wide in functionalist accounts that its usefulness is, eventually, questionable.

The purpose of Cavanaugh's argument is to challenge the distinction between the categories of 'religious' and 'secular'. He argues that 'religion' is not to be thought of as a feature of human life with a fixed and immutable meaning. It is, rather, a construction on which the 'myth of religious violence' is founded. Far from being a universal and timeless feature of human existence, religion is "a contingent power arrangement of the modern west."[40] Perpetuation of the myth allows the secular nation-state to be thought of as an enduring and timeless guardian against the inherent dangers of religion.

The myth of religious violence tries to establish as timeless, universal, and natural a very contingent set of categories — religious and secular — that are in fact constructions of the modern West. Those who do not accept these categories as timeless, universal and natural are subject to coercion.[41]

This ideological construction of 'religion', Cavanaugh argues, allows certain forms of power to be authorised by the secular nation-state in order to marginalise religion from public discourse and consolidate public allegiance to the state.

In advancing his thesis about the 'myth' of religious violence, Cavanaugh's primary concern is not so much with moral scrutiny of violent actions committed by people who subscribe to the doctrines of Christianity or Islam. Nor does he offer a theory of religion and violence. His aim, by disproving the notion that the categories of 'religion' and 'secular' are trans-historical and timeless, is to show how the myth of religious violence serves to divert such scrutiny from other kinds of discourse and action:

> The idea that public religion causes violence authorises the marginalisation of those things called religion from having a divisive influence in public life, and thereby authorises the state's monopoly on violence and public allegiance.[42]

Moral scrutiny, accordingly, is directed at 'religious' forms of violence and away from 'secular' forms:

> Loyalty to one's religion is private in origin and therefore optional; loyalty to the secular nation-state is what unifies us and is not optional. The problem with the myth of religious violence is not that it condemns certain kinds of violence, but that it diverts moral scrutiny from other kinds of violence.[43]

A reconsidered understanding of the categories of 'religious' and 'secular' should lead us to abandon the myth of religious violence. Once the myth has been exposed, proper attention can be given both to the power exercised by the state and to the ways the exercise of such power is justified.

Cavanaugh makes a significant argument about the importance of expanding the scope of moral scrutiny. Bringing light to bear on how the nation-state authorises its use of violence does, indeed, weaken the claim that were it not for the scourge of religion, humankind would live freed from the constraints of theistic tyranny in realms of Elysian peace.

Cavanaugh wants to cease categorising violence as either religious or secular.[44] Instead, the root of all violence should be considered ideological. In setting aside the religious/secular divide, Cavanaugh seeks to direct efforts towards finding the true, deep roots of conflict:

> Rather than attempt to come up with reasons that a universal and timeless feature of human society called religion has a peculiar tendency to promote violence, the question for researchers would be: under what circumstances do ideologies and practices of all kinds promote violence?[45]

The importance of Cavanaugh's analysis is that it exposes the idea that "there is something in the world that we understand to be religion and this thing is violent" as historically and philosophically questionable.[46] It is a foundational mistake and should make us more guarded about assuming that, if religion is inherently violent, any intervention of the liberal, secular state against religion is bound always to be just.

It is not part of Cavanaugh's argument that acts of religious violence do *not* occur. They do, and he acknowledges this. What he questions is the conventional categorical distinction between 'religious' and 'secular' and, with it, the assumed primacy of the latter over the former. For Cavanaugh, the moral quality of violence perpetrated in the name of God is of the same order as that perpetrated in the name of the state; and, indeed, he holds that 'secular' is as much an ideological term as 'religious'.

Nonetheless, when confronted by situations where violent, religious ideological threats are made, the liberal, secular state, accustomed to ideological neutrality, is bound to have to make some form of intervention. A key obligation of the state is to protect and strengthen society, but might its own studied neutrality hinder its capacity to discharge this obligation? It is important to consider what kind of response a liberal state should appropriately make in circumstances marked by deep ideological disagreement.

Religion and the secular state: Can the phoenix of tolerance fly again?

Secular critics of religion often ignore the religious claims on which those who kill in the name of God base their actions. They do so because they dismiss the claims either as nonsense or as so inherently violent as to be lacking any moral merit.

Such a dismissal, however, represents, at the least, a failure to take seriously the fact that when religious actors claim to be acting in the name of their faith, they mean precisely that. If we fail to take seriously such claims, how well will we be equipped to address the issue? As Susan Mendus has written:

> My hunch is that modern liberals do not have an accurate understanding of religiously motivated acts of violence and that very fact makes them more vulnerable to religiously motivated terrorist attacks. [They] have a tendency to reduce religious actions to political actions, but the former are not reducible to the latter and this is a fact which we ignore at our peril.[47]

Although liberals like to speak about the merits of pluralism, Mendus is concerned that "modern liberal political theory fails to take seriously the depth of disagreement that divides people in modern societies and, in particular, fails to take seriously the distinctive character of religious belief."[48] She insists religious actions are not reducible to political actions, and must be understood on their own terms.

At the heart of liberalism lies a recognition that reasonable people will disagree, sometimes permanently, and even irreconcilably, about their conceptions of the 'good life'. Yet toleration of disagreement is a feature of liberalism that is not necessarily reciprocated by other political philosophies. Liberalism is a response to the reality of reasonable disagreement founding the principles of political association upon a core morality.

Political philosopher Charles Larmore[49] uses the term 'reasonableness' to refer to the capacity to exercise reason in an area of enquiry but notes that it has "ceased to seem a guarantee of ultimate agreement about deep questions concerning how we should live."[50]

Susan Mendus

My hunch is that modern liberals do not have an accurate understanding of religiously motivated acts of violence and that very fact makes them more vulnerable to religiously motivated terrorist attacks. [They] have a tendency to reduce religious actions to political actions, but the former are not reducible to the latter and this is a fact which we ignore at our peril.

What does liberalism have to say concerning this absence of agreement about the sources of value? Liberalism does not *affirm* differences between people but simply acknowledges that the *existence* of disagreement is predictable; but it is a prediction founded on the assumption that the religious and the political are completely separate. Mendus believes, correctly, that this is a mistake.

John Locke's defence of toleration is usually invoked as the basis on which a modern liberal society accepts differences between those holding different points of view. Locke, however, did not draw a distinction between the religious and political in the way that contemporary thinkers do.

Locke's argument "sought to persuade religious believers that politics should distance itself from religious matters because God (*their* God) wished it to be so. For Locke, the tolerant state acquired both its authority and its scope from God Himself." [Italics in original][51] Modern conceptions of liberalism, by contrast, simply assert a clear distinction between religion and politics.

The clarity of that distinction, however, may be more apparent than real. Just as Cavanaugh argued, in exposing the myth that violence can be described as specifically 'religious', so, too, Mendus argues, there are important implications to be drawn from the fact that the line between the religious and the political is not as clear as is often assumed:

> It may be the case that what we see as political is not thought of in that way by the agents themselves, and indeed it may be inflammatory to insist on construing as political what is seen by the actors themselves as religious. [Modern liberalism] simply assumes that we know what counts as political, and that we know the political has priority.[52]

When coming to terms with the phenomenon of religious violence, the liberal state must not make the mistake of treating the religious as the political. It must recognise "the status of religious as a thing in itself, distinct from, and sometimes in conflict with politics."[53] Is the liberal state, in addition, able to recognise that sometimes this conflict will lead the faithful to assert the primacy of religious law over secular law? How is a secular state to respond to such an assertion?

Meeting Antigone's challenge: when the laws of God override the laws of the state

Religious actors who resort to violence are almost certainly expressing a rejection of secular, liberal norms of belief and conduct. Modern liberals tend to assume that, if a religious individual is asked to weigh political and religious considerations against each other, the scales will tip in favour of the political.

One response to the claim that our reasons to be liberal will always tip towards the political has been traced back to Sophocles, in *Antigone*.[54] When Antigone explains to her uncle, King Creon, why she disobeyed his law forbidding her to bury her brother, she says: "Nor did I think your edict had such force that you, a mere mortal, could override the gods, the great unwritten, unshakable traditions."

For political scientists, Matthew Clayton and David Stevens, this response is of decisive importance: where the two conflict, according to Antigone, the laws of the gods override the laws of a liberal society. Clayton and Stevens argue that, given the eternal nature of the believer's relationship with God, and the high stakes that turn on obedience to God's law, it is hard to believe liberal political authority would prevail for the believer who found herself in conflict with the state.

What response, then, is to be made to the believer who accords more weight to the religious than to the political? The error often made by the modern liberal, as Mendus notes, is to assume the religious must be understood as, in fact, the political. Clayton and Stevens agree with her about this mistaken assumption. The appropriate response, they argue, is to say that the believer is wrong on *religious* rather than political grounds:

> We must say that the believer's religious views are
> mistaken as political views, rather than mistaken in
> treating them as having more weight than they do.
> Because her religious views are mistaken they do not
> give the believer a reason not to support and comply with
> constitutional liberal arrangements.[55]

Who is to make such a response to the non-compliant religious believer and challenge their conception of religion? Clayton and Stevens argue that if politicians respond, they risk losing widespread support from citizens and, by weakening consensus, threatening their legitimate authority. They propose, instead, that the task of challenging unreasonable religious actions or teachings be delegated to citizens themselves — and, in particular, to those who share the same doctrinal beliefs:

> Reasonable religious citizens might, as part of the natural
> duty of justice, be permitted — perhaps even morally
> required in certain circumstances — to explain to fellow
> believers, including non-compliant believers, why religious
> belief is compatible with, or supports liberal norms. Not
> engaging with the religiously unreasonable may carry
> significant costs for the liberal project of fostering support
> for a conception of justice, and liberals also have a duty to
> be evangelical about their political morality.[56]

The key point in the argument is that challenges from the unreasonable, religious non-compliant must be addressed in *theological* rather than political terms. The criticism levelled earlier by Mendus against political liberals — that they often fail to accept that religious actors really are acting in the name of religion — is echoed by Clayton and Stevens. Political liberalism is not a free-standing conception: "instead, [it] may, at times, be more accurately described as a partially comprehensive conception."[57] Liberalism needs to recognise the reality of that partial conception, and to take religion seriously.

On keeping the peace: religious belief and rational choice

Taking religion seriously does not mean compromising ideological neutrality. Indeed, if Jonathan Sacks is correct, the liberal state has no business whatsoever in trying to embody truth, goodness or beauty. It may, however, have some business in not embodying falsehood, evil or ugliness. The state's function is to aspire to keep the peace between contending factions. Liberalism "is procedural rather than substantive," says Sacks. "It makes no claim to represent the totality of life."[58]

Government action in the face of terror attacks waged by religious extremists is often accompanied by renewed calls from politicians, journalists and academics, among others, for certain extremist religious groups, such as Hizb ut-Tahrir, to be banned (Hizb ut-Tahrir is, in fact, banned in the UK). In addition, there are calls for an entire and coherent system of religious belief to reform itself and embrace the Enlightenment principles according to which most Westerners are accustomed to live.[59]

But banning organisations accomplishes little other than to heighten their attractiveness in certain quarters; and waiting for a reform-minded Muslim cleric to post a series of theses urging significant doctrinal reform can best be described as a long shot — probably also entailing a long wait. Yet the problem of religious violence remains: extremists kill those whom they believe are the enemies of God, and they hold to theologies that sanction such violence.

Acts of extremist violence are criminal acts and need to be punished by applying the sanctions of the criminal law. But violence is only one manifestation of religious extremism. Radical religious views may be espoused that conflict directly with the prevailing norms — and laws — of wider society.

This happened in April 2017 when the Australian branch of Hizb ut-Tahrir released a video claiming it was acceptable in Islam for a husband to hit his wife in a 'managed' way.[60]

The video was widely criticised by Muslims and non-Muslims alike, and a debate erupted about whether the *Qu'ran* does or does not sanction striking. Soon enough, calls were also made for some kind of action, albeit unspecified, to be taken.[61]

When governments develop policies aimed at changing the attitudes and behaviours of religious extremists, they generally intend to forestall future acts of violence. But are these policies sound?

Economists Lawrence Iannaccone[62] and Eli Berman[63] have questioned conventional government responses to the threat posed by religious extremism to civil society. They base their analysis, and the policy conclusions they draw from it, on the economics of the religious marketplace and contend that the behaviour of religious extremists must be viewed as rational — that is, as normal and reasonable.[64] It is a serious mistake, they write, "to view religious extremists as pathological drones enslaved by the theologies of hate."[65] Implications for the responses made by governments to extremist behaviour flow from this analysis:

> To label religious extremism the product of ignorance, coercion or psychopathology is to foster misunderstanding. To combat extremism (as opposed to extremist violence) with the powers of the state is to invite conflict if that extremism represents a widespread unmet demand for some set of services. To support 'good' religion while repressing 'bad' religion is to invite violence.[66]

In any case, as Iannaccone and Berman note, religious belief systems that have been successful in binding their members in cooperative and supportive agreement are very difficult to refute. It is insufficient to argue that a belief system is untrue or wrong or misguided; what committed believer will be dissuaded by that?

Successful religious groups consolidate their positions by

supplying essential goods, such as health care and education with great efficiency. For example, this is part of the appeal of, and widespread support for, Hamas in Gaza. The presence of strong, constitutional democracy, together with a healthy market economy, is one way to undercut the political appeal of such sects and reduce the incidence of religious violence:

> Religious radicals are less likely to flourish and less likely to embrace violence when there is strong competition in their non-core markets: including education, health care, poverty programs, and political representation.[67]

Similar principles of religious competition to reduce religious violence can be applied in countries that already enjoy established constitutional democracies and vibrant market economies. Competition between sects in the religious marketplace, argue Iannaccone and Berman, can be effective in inducing moderation. Reduction in state support for religion makes a nation's religious market much more open to entry and competition, and is accompanied by a reduction in the political activities of denominations. Why?

Because the stakes have been lowered? In the absence of the prize of government money and protection from competing groups, a religion finds political activity much less attractive. Open competition also leads to more groups, each of which has less capacity to influence government.[68]

Viewing religious behaviour as an instance of rational choice, as Iannaccone and Berman contend, can help to reframe responses to religious violence. Instead of seeing the option for religious violence as an aberrant and irrational form of behaviour, choosing violence is better thought of as a rational act that has desirable consequences for the actors — whether in the form of social esteem, supernatural vindication, or existential purpose.

Can governments address this rational behaviour by targeting beliefs and teachings? The response of Iannacone and Berman is, no. Secular attacks convince no one and merely serve to antagonise many. Hence the futility of political leaders declaiming on the authenticity or inauthenticity of Islamic theology. "Indeed, if anyone is equipped to win theological debates with radical sectarians, it is leaders of *other* religious groups" [Italics in original].[69]

Confronting religious violence in a liberal society

Committed in the name of God, religiously motivated acts of terror continue to present a growing threat to liberal democracies. The religious factor has, indeed, been among the most perplexing elements in these horrific occurrences for citizens in countries such as Belgium, Spain, Germany, the United Kingdom, the United States, and Australia — nations long accustomed to the conventions of tolerance, pluralism and liberty.

These violent actions are not a new phenomenon; what has changed is the experience citizens of Western democracies, except in some measure, the United States, now have of those actions, whether as witnesses or victims.

Western societies feel themselves to be under increasing threat from those determined to destroy liberal societies. Writing in response to the terrorist attack in London in March 2017, Daniel Johnson observed that:

> The bloodbath on Westminster Bridge and at the Houses of Parliament is the price we pay for failing to instil the values of [Western] civilisation into all those who claim the right to call themselves British citizens.[70]

Australia faces a similar threat, albeit on a smaller scale, where there is, in addition, an incidental and growing problem as some teenagers choose to express their individuality by committing — or threatening to commit — brutal terrorist attacks.

Recent reports indicate more than half of the investigations carried out by the Australian Security Intelligence Organisation are directed at people aged 25 years and younger: three times what it was a few years ago. Intelligence agencies are working hard to tap into teenagers' social media networks, and governments are putting a lot of money behind them.

The growth of Islamic extremism, especially in public schools, is confronting governments with a significant problem because no one knows quite what to do. The challenge for 'de-radicalisation' programs intended to help schools to counter extremist behaviour, such as the NSW Government's *School Communities Working Together* program, is complex. As yet, there is little evidence that complying with the government's de-radicalisation guidelines will make it less likely that extremist acts will occur. No single program has successfully turned a radicalised teen back to being a good citizen.

Dislodging deadly ideas, whether from the heads of teenagers or from the heads of other kinds of religious extremist, requires more than government programs or stern speeches from political leaders.

Part of the problem, as already identified, is that a pluralist society lacks a "providential ordering of the universe."[71] There are many understandings of truth, and some religious extremists are prepared to kill in the name of that truth; but government in a liberal society can have no part in arbitrating between different conceptions of truth.

Responding to religious violence needs the determined effort of all citizens, especially those with responsibility for leading religious communities. In describing the features of a liberal society, British commentators Richard Koch and Chris Smith are unequivocal:

> Liberal societies are marked by freedom of religion and conscience, openness, widespread tolerance, the ability to collaborate, and the willingness of citizens to take responsibility for their actions. Liberal societies are tolerant of new or unusual behaviour because there is a sense of common membership and identity uniting even the most disparate groups.[72]

There are no obvious answers to the problem of religious

violence. Although it is not a new phenomenon, it has taken on a new, more deadly form that is provoking heightened concerns about the integration of Muslims into the wider society. In response to these concerns, it is clear governments must act to secure the safety of citizens. But draconian and illiberal measures, provoked by fear, should not be what guides political responses to religious violence as these can further harden and entrench extremist behaviour.

"War is the enemy of liberal values," Koch and Smith insist. "Terrorists win when we abandon the very principles of justice and democracy we are seeking to defend."[73] Even under severe provocation, it is important for a liberal society to maintain a sense of proportion and to uphold the fundamental principle of equality under the rule of secular law for all citizens. A liberal society must tackle hostile views directly and not by suppression of rights and civil liberties.

Efforts to preserve what Koch and Smith describe as "a sense of underlying common identity and purpose" must include a renewed commitment to upholding the right to religious liberty, removing restrictions on freedom of speech (a key manifestation of freedom of conscience) — and emphatically resisting calls to introduce religious belief as a ground for complaint in anti-discrimination legislation.[74]

Confronting religious violence effectively requires preservation of strong bonds of trust and respect between citizens, the voluntary associations of civil society, among them religious communities, and the organs of government. It also requires an unfailing commitment to upholding the cultural, moral, and legal stability of a liberal society in order that citizens may freely challenge religious believers who advocate militant or illiberal teachings.

Encouraging an open and vigorous exchange of religious ideas, including criticism of doctrine, without fear of attack or legal action, will not eliminate the threat of religious violence; but it will temper and moderate the environment in which religious violence incubates.

Upholding and defending the principles of an open, liberal society needs to be a priority for all who are prepared to engage in the philosophical contest provoked by religious violence. Citizens of liberal societies must learn to take religion, and the claims of religious believers, seriously, just as the beliefs and convictions of adherents of secular ideologies should similarly be addressed. Those who place their ultimate trust and hope in God do so already.

As this essay was being composed, two terrorist attacks were launched in England within as many weeks. The slaughter caused by a suicide bomber in the foyer of a Manchester arena, and then by three men armed with knives and using a truck in a busy area of south London, proves once again that jihadi terrorists will stop at nothing to destroy our way of life. Only week or so after the Lindt Café siege inquiry handed down its report, we were faced, yet again, with authorities scrambling to make sense of sadistic destruction of innocent lives.[75]

Islamic State swiftly claimed responsibility for both attacks in England, lauding the actions of "soldiers of the Caliphate" and warning in videos that "there is more to come". Indeed, the three London attackers were heard to cry, "This is for Allah", as they stabbed their victims, thereby proclaiming the religious meaning behind their attack. The pattern in Manchester and Southwark is now only too familiar from other atrocities committed by Islamist terrorists around the world. Random, deadly attacks launched against ordinary members of the society are becoming commonplace in Western democracies.

The then British Home Secretary, Amber Rudd, was quick to condemn the Manchester explosion as a "barbaric act"; and, following the London slayings, Theresa May, then Prime Minister of the United Kingdom, declared, "Enough is enough" — although she appeared to be hardening her stance towards extremism in general and not only towards Islamism. But, despite the connection established between these attackers and radical Islam, there is a grave danger politicians will go out of their way to explain the terrorists were not, and could not have been, acting in the name of Islam. Islam and barbarism are incompatible, they are likely to tell us.

Fear of being branded 'Islamophobic' stifles many politicians, journalists, and community leaders from criticising Islam. They prefer to say attacks are a 'perversion' of Islam. But, as this essay has argued, a harder question is whether jihadist violence actually has deep doctrinal, scriptural, and historical roots in mainstream Islam. There is great pressure to avoid asking that question.

Whatever the *Qu'ran* actually says about violence, it is clear Islam provides an ideological framework giving suicidal psychopaths the sense of purpose that motivates them to act. Jihadist attacks perpetrated by so-called 'lone wolf' killers — who intend to slaughter as many people as possible — almost invariably end with the death of the attacker. This is not an accident.

The terrorist's death is not an unfortunate consequence of his or her action: it is a central part of the plan. Jihadists choose death and are determined to die. Their aim is rejection, not reform. As one expert on political Islam and Islamist terrorism has written: "Violence is not a means. It is an end in itself. It is violence devoid of a future."[76] We struggle to understand what drives an individual — usually male, often young, and with their whole life before them — to perpetrate such nihilistic and suicidal atrocities.

Acts of terror committed in the name of Islam pose a serious dilemma for Western countries long accustomed to a political and social ethos of tolerance and liberty. The terrorists hold the upper hand: security services simply cannot keep track of everyone who is of concern. Arrests frequently follow an attack, thereby forestalling further attacks; preventing an attack from occurring in the first place is much more difficult. Shortly after the Manchester attack, police in Adelaide detained a 22-year old Somali-Australian woman who has been charged with being a member of Islamic State. But for every suspect apprehended, many more are likely to slip through the net.

What is to be done? Ramping up security in all public arenas will continue but, in reality, it offers only limited protection – until the next attack, followed by yet more thorough measures. Dislodging violent ideas from the heads of death-obsessed religious extremists needs more than imposing further bag checks or telling those being attacked to: "Run, Hide, Tell."

It means renewing our commitment to liberty, tolerance, and the rule of law. It means reclaiming the principles of Western civilisation, fostering them in every citizen, and working hard to ensure newcomers to a country are integrated into the wider society. It also means encouraging open discussion about religious ideas — including criticism of religion — without fear of attack or legal action under the guise of stamping out 'Islamophobia'.

This is not a quick-fix solution. It will take a long time, and it will not eliminate the threat of religious violence altogether. But it will temper the environment in which such violence breeds. Religious violence is provoking a deadly contest about fundamental beliefs. Each one of us is now engaged in that contest — and we need to be clear about what it is we must defend.

REFERENCES

1   Martha C. Nussbaum, *The New Religious Intolerance: Overcoming the Politics of Fear in an Anxious Age* (Cambridge MA: Belknap Press, 2012), 19.

2   Griff Witte, "London terror attack: no evidence Khalid Masood was linked to Islamic State", *Sydney Morning Herald* (28 March 2017).

3   Jon Stone, "Theresa May says it's wrong to describe London attack as 'Islamic terrorism'", *The Independent* (23 March 2017).

4   I am grateful to Professor Clive Kessler for emphasising this point. "The critical question that politicians are all too eager to avoid is whether 'Islamism' is a misappropriation of Islam or whether it has deep and authenticating textual, doctrinal, and historical roots in mainstream Islam. That is the key issue that has to be faced.

There are great political pressures these days not to do so." (Private correspondence with the author, 13 May 2017.)

5 Matt Ridley, "Stand up for the right to criticise Islam", *The Times* (27 March 2017).

6 A word about terminology is in order: the term, 'religious violence', will be used in this essay to refer specifically to violent physical acts claimed to be motivated by religious beliefs, teachings or doctrines. It is a term with a very broad application. When violent acts are perpetrated in the name religion, it may be the case that other social and political factors have contributed to the disturbance. Although 'terrorism' is widely held to refer to violent action in pursuit of secular, political objectives, when those objectives are religious, it is appropriate to refer to acts of 'religious terrorism'. As for the meaning of 'violence', this essay defines it as "behavior involving physical force intended to hurt, damage, or kill someone or something."

7 Jonathan Sacks (b. 1948), a British Orthodox rabbi, theologian, and writer, was Chief Rabbi of the United Hebrew Congregations of the Commonwealth from 1991 to 2013.

8 Jonathan Sacks, *Not in God's Name: Confronting Religious Violence* (London: Hodder & Stoughton, 2015), 39.

9 Susan Mendus is a political philosopher and Professor Emerita of Political Philosophy at the University of York, UK.

10 Susan Mendus, "Religious Tolerance and Religious Violence", *Bijdragen, International Journal in Philosophy and Theology* (2010), 71(4), 426-437, 432.

11 Jonathan Sacks, *Not in God's Name: Confronting Religious Violence* (London: Hodder & Stoughton, 2015), 229.

12 This section draws significantly on Mark Juergensmeyer, "Religious Violence", in Michael Jerryson, Mark Juergensmeyer, and Margo Kitts, (eds), *The Oxford Handbook of Religion and Violence* (Oxford: Oxford University Press, 2013), online version.

13 Mark Juergensmeyer, "Religious Violence", as above.

14 Steve Clarke is an Australian philosopher based at the Centre for Applied Philosophy and Public Ethics at Charles Sturt University.

15 Steve Clarke, *The Justification of Religious Violence* (Chichester: Wiley-Blackwell, 2014), 19.

16 See, for example, Alan Mittleman, "The Problem of Religious Violence", *Political Theology*, Vol. 12.5 (2011), 722-726, 722.

17 Scott Thomas is a political scientist based at the University of Bath, UK.

18 Scott Thomas, "A Globalized God: Religion's Growing Influence in International Politics", *Foreign Affairs*, Vol. 89 No. 6 (November/December 2010), 98. See also, Laurence Iannaccone and Eli Berman,

"Religious extremism: The good, the bad, and the deadly", *Public Choice* (2006) 128: 109-129.

19 Scott Thomas, as above, 98.

20 Mark Juergensmeyer is a scholar in sociology and religious studies based at the University of California Santa Barbara where he is Distinguished Professor of Sociology and Global Studies. He is best known for his research on religious violence.

21 Mark Juergensmeyer, "Religious Violence", as above.

22 Daniel Philpott is Professor of Political Science at the University of Notre Dame, and a scholar of religion and global politics.

23 Daniel Philpott, "Religion and Violence from a Political Science Perspective", in Michael Jerryson, Mark Juergensmeyer, and Margo Kitts, (eds), *The Oxford Handbook of Religion and Violence* (Oxford: Oxford University Press, 2013), online version. See also Monica Toft, Daniel Philpott, and Timothy Shah, (eds), *God's Century: Resurgent Religion and Global Politics* (New York: W.W. Norton, 2011), 121-147.

24 Daniel Philpott, as above, 8. See also the note about terminology in footnote 4.

25 Daniel Philpott, as above, 8.

26 Daniel Philpott, as above, 9.

27 Liam Stack, "A Brief History of Deadly Attacks on Abortion Providers", *The New York Times* (29 November 2015).

28 Liam Stack, as above.

29 Mark Juergensmeyer, "Religious Violence", in Michael Jerryson, Mark Juergensmeyer, and Margo Kitts, (eds), *The Oxford Handbook of Religion and Violence* (Oxford: Oxford University Press, 2013), online version.

30 Mark Juergensmeyer and Mona Sheikh, "A Sociotheological Approach to Understanding Religious Violence", in Michael Jerryson, Mark Juergensmeyer, and Margo Kitts, (eds), *The Oxford Handbook of Religion and Violence* (Oxford: Oxford University Press, 2013), online version.

31 Alan Mittleman, as above, 732.

32 Raymond Ibrahim, "Why is Easter a Magnet for Islamist Violence?", Middle East Forum (17 April 2017). See also, Raymond Ibrahim, *Crucified Again: Exposing Islam's New War on Christians* (Washington DC: Regnery, 2013).

33 Sam Harris, *The End of Faith: Religion, Terror, and the Future of Reason,* (New York: W.W. Norton, 2005), 27.

34 William Cavanaugh (b. 1962) is a Roman Catholic theologian best known for his work in political theology and Christian ethics. Based at DePaul University, Illinois, he is author of *The Myth of Religious Violence: Secular Ideology and the Roots of Modern Conflict*, published in 2009.

35 William Cavanaugh, *The Myth of Religious Violence: Secular Ideology and the Roots of Modern Conflict* (New York, NY: Oxford University Press, 2009), 85.

36 William Cavanaugh, *The Myth of Religious Violence*, as above, 121.

37 William Cavanaugh, *The Myth of Religious Violence*, as above, 105.

38 William Cavanaugh, *The Myth of Religious Violence*, as above, 109.

39 William Cavanaugh, *The Myth of Religious Violence*, as above, 118.

40 William Cavanaugh, *The Myth of Religious Violence*, as above, 17.

41 William Cavanaugh, *The Myth of Religious Violence*, as above, 6.

42 William Cavanaugh, *The Myth of Religious Violence*, as above, 121.

43 Willliam Cavanaugh, *The Myth of Religious Violence*, as above, 121.

44 See, Debra Erickson, Review, *The Journal of Religion* Vol. 90, No. 4 (October 2010), 582-584.

45 William Cavanaugh, *The Myth of Religious Violence*, as above, 226.

46 Kevin O'Neill, Review, *Journal of Church and State*, Vol. 52, No. 1 (Winter 2010), 164-165.

47 Susan Mendus, "Religious Tolerance and Religious Violence", as above, 427-8.

48 Susan Mendus, "Religious Tolerance and Religious Violence", as above, 428.

49 Charles Larmore, a philosopher known for his work on political liberalism, is based at Brown University, Rhode Island.

50 Charles Larmore, "Pluralism and Reasonable Disagreement", *Social Philosophy and Policy* (1994) Vol. 11(1), 61-79, 74.

51 Susan Mendus, "Religious Tolerance and Religious Violence", as above, 435.

52 Susan Mendus, "Religious Tolerance", as above, 435-6.

53 Susan Mendus, "Religious Tolerance", as above, 436.

54 Matthew Clayton and David Stevens, "When God Commands Disobedience: Political Liberalism and Unreasonable Religions", *Res Publica* (2014) 20:65-84, 77.

55 Matthew Clayton and David Stevens, "When God Commands Disobedience", as above, 79.

56 Matthew Clayton and David Stevens, "When God Commands Disobedience", as above, 81, 83.

57 Matthew Clayton and David Stevens, "When God Commands Disobedience", as above, 83.

58 Jonathan Sacks, *Not in God's Name: Confronting Religious Violence* (London: Hodder & Stoughton, 2015), as above, 229.

59 See, for example, Ayan Hirsi Ali, *Heretic: Why Islam Needs a Reformation Now* (New York: HarperCollins, 2015), 3: "Without fundamental alterations to some of Islam's core concepts, I believe, we shall not

solve the burning and increasingly global problem of political violence carried out in the name of religion."

60 Rachel Baxendale, "Domestic violence is not a beautiful blessing", *The Australian* (13 April 2017); Rachel Olding, "Muslim men permitted to hit wives in a soft and 'symbolic' way, Hizb ut-Tahrir Australia women say", *Sydney Morning Herald* (13 April 2017). See also Bernard Lagan, "You can hit your wife gently, Muslims told", *The Times* (14 April 2017).

61 Caroline Overington, "This is something we must confront right here, right now", *The Australian* (15 April 2017).

62 Laurence Iannaccone, Professor of Economics at Chapman University in California, is a pioneer in the field of economics of religion which applies economic insights to religion and religious practice.

63 Eli Berman, Professor of Economics at the University of California San Diego, is known for application of rational choice analysis to the behaviour of radical religious groups.

64 Laurence Iannacone and Eli Berman, "Religious extremism: The good, the bad, and the deadly", *Public Choice* (2006) 128: 109-129, 111.

65 Laurence Iannaccone and Eli Berman, "Religious extremism", as above, 123.

66 Laurence Iannaccone and Eli Berman, "Religious extremism", as above, 111.

67 Laurence Iannaccone and Eli Berman, "Religious extremism", as above, 124.

68 Laurence Iannaccone and Eli Berman, "Religious extremism", as above, 122-3.

69 Laurence Iannaccone and Eli Berman, "Religious extremism", as above, 123.

70 Daniel Johnson, "Not tweets and anger, but redoubled vigilance", *Standpoint* (April 2017), 21.

71 See footnote 6, above.

72 Richard Koch and Chris Smith, *Suicide of the West* (London: Continuum, 2006), 113, 114.

73 Richard Koch and Chris Smith, *Suicide of the West* as above, 126.

74 Richard Koch and Chris Smith, *Suicide of the West* as above, 131.

75 See, State Coroner of New South Wales, Inquest into the deaths arising from the Lindt Café siege: findings and recommendations (May 2017). See also Deborah Snow, *Siege: Inside the Lindt Café* (Crows Nest, NSW: Allen & Unwin, 2018).

76 Olivier Roy, *Jihad and Death: The Global Appeal of Islamic State* (London: Hurst, 2017), 2.

8

ANTI-ZIONISM
AND THE POSTMODERN LEFT

From anti-racism to antisemitism

Antisemitism has mutated from prejudice against Jews as people to prejudice against Jews as a people.[1]

Antisemitism – the ancient hatred with us still

Campaigning in the 2019 Australian federal election was marred by a number of ugly antisemitic incidents. The campaign corflutes of three Jewish candidates, Julian Leeser, Jason Falinski, and Josh Frydenberg – all of whom were sitting Liberal MPs – were defaced with dollar signs, devil's horns, and Hitler moustaches. Antisemitic emails also were directed at another Jewish candidate, Kerryn Phelps; and posters displayed by Dave Sharma, a non-Jewish candidate campaigning in an electorate with a large number of Jewish voters, were also defaced.[2]

Remarking on the campaign after he had been re-elected, Julian Leeser observed that it had been, "singularly the dirtiest and nastiest election I can remember. It really left a disgusting feeling. It's so un-Australian."[3] Such blatant eruption of antisemitism in Australia took many by surprise and was widely condemned. But the warning signs had been apparent to many observers for some time.

The Executive Council of Australian Jewry produces an annual report assessing the state of antisemitism in Australia. In its report published in 2010, Jeremy Jones observed that "Australia does not have a past to which anti-Semites can comfortably look with nostalgia, which distinguishes it from many other countries."[4]

Nonetheless, the 2010 report noted a culture tolerant of antisemitism in Australia that "has been exacerbated with the growing phenomenon of anti-Semitism purporting to be representative of a left-wing or 'anti-racist' opinion." It is a phenomenon which, according to Jones, is extremely difficult to measure.[5]

The 2018 report presented a somewhat bleaker picture, recording 366 antisemitic incidents – an increase of 59 per cent over the previous twelve month period:

> Many of the principal themes in these expressions of antisemitism, especially online, involve a cross-fertilisation of concepts between the political Left and Right. For example, left-wing rhetoric exaggerating the power of a so-called 'Jewish lobby' has helped to revive and stoke far-right myths about a world Jewish conspiracy or of Jews controlling the media, economy, government or other societal institutions.[6]

Spelling antisemitism

There are different points of view about the correct spelling of *antisemitism*. Some opt for anti-Semitism; others for Anti-Semitism; while others adopt Antisemitism. The problem with using a hyphen in the spelling is that 'anti-Semitism' suggests that one is opposed to 'Semitism'. But this is an artificial construct: when Wilhelm Marr, a journalist, coined the term, *Antisemitismus*, in the 19th century, he was directing his animus specifically towards Jews, whom he hated. As Deborah Lipstadt[7] has argued:

> In my own English-language usage I choose not to go with the hyphen because the word, both as its creator had intended and as it has been generally used for the past

one hundred and fifty years, means, quite simply, the hatred of Jews.[8]

The International Holocaust Remembrance Alliance (IHRA), a large, multinational intergovernmental body, has advocated strongly for adoption of *antisemitism* as the correct spelling on the basis that it should be read as "a unified term so that the meaning of the generic term for modern Jew-hatred is clear."[9]

This essay will adopt the spelling advocated by IHRA and Lipstadt: *antisemitism*. Where, however, a particular author who uses a different form (such as 'anti-Semitism') is quoted, the essay will retain the spelling preferred by that author.

New forms of the ancient hatred

Antisemitism – the hatred of Jews – is an ancient hatred, long a part of human history, which has appeared in different forms, with different motivations, and with varying intensities. It is also a hatred that has been defined in widely varying ways.

In 2016 the IHRA adopted a "Working Definition of Antisemitism" that has now become the most widely accepted definition. It is the definition used in this essay:

> Antisemitism is a certain perception of Jews, which may be expressed as hatred toward Jews. Rhetorical and physical manifestations of antisemitism are directed toward Jewish or non-Jewish individuals and/or their property, toward Jewish community institutions and religious facilities.[10]

There are many explanations for antisemitism. It predates the advent of Christianity but there is, nonetheless, a view that it is Christianity that provides "the foundational antisemitic paradigm" by creating an understanding of Jewishness as the inimical opposite of Christianity.[11]

The vast demonology about Jews created, in part, by Christianity became – and remains – deeply entrenched in Western culture. The conceptual structure of this paradigm is that Jews are noxious, malevolent, powerful, dangerous, and different. It is a view of Jews that provokes an eliminationist response which is an integral component of antisemitism. As Jonathan Sacks[12] has noted:

> Antisemitism exists and is dangerous whenever two contradictory factors appear in combination: the belief that Jews are so powerful that they are responsible for the evils of the world, and the knowledge that they are so powerless that they can be attacked with impunity.[13]

After the Second World War and the Holocaust, antisemitism seemed unthinkable. Any public expression of antisemitism was certainly unacceptable; however, it was not so easy to dissipate views about Jews that people held in private. There is now plenty of evidence that whatever views are held in private, *public* expressions of antisemitism are rising again in many parts of the Western world.

Writing in the *Philadelphia Inquirer* in August 2019, Marc Thiessen cited a recent CNN poll which found that "more than a quarter of Europeans say Jews have too much influence in business and finance, while one in five said Jews have too much influence in the media and politics."[14] In a survey of Israeli Jews conducted in 2016, the Pew Research Center found that 64 per cent of those surveyed thought antisemitism was very common around the world in total; but 76 per cent thought antisemitism is not only common but is increasing.[15]

In global terms, antisemitism has spread with the greatest intensity in Arab and Islamic countries during the post-war era. The establishment of the State of Israel in 1948 contributed to this intensification; but it also coincided with the rise of Arab nationalism and emergence of anti-colonialist sentiment in Europe. But it must necessarily be stressed, strongly, that antisemitism is neither a consequence of the existence of Israel nor of its actions.

Antisemitism's tropes are age-old and precede Israel's founding, its conflict with the Palestinians, and its dealings with its Arab neighbours. In Daniel Jonah Goldhagen's[16] words: "Israel's conduct does not affect the incidence of antisemitism in general, which is grounded in deep-seated and long-standing orientations, emotions, and beliefs."[17] Nor does existence of antisemitism depend upon the actions of Jews, whether individually or collectively.[18]

In the countries of Western Europe there has been a decline in public manifestations of antisemitism; open expression of race-based prejudice remains unacceptable. Racial antisemitism has, in the past, frequently been associated with the political right. In the past forty or fifty years, however, a distinctive form of non-racial antisemitism has emerged as a potent force on the political left – what is frequently called the 'postmodern left'. Robert Wistrich[19] has charted this evolution:

> Classical anti-Semitism, it should be remembered, proclaimed the Jews as a minority group to be an existential menace to a given nation—a danger to its internal homogeneity, unity, religious values, and racial purity. Postwar anti-Zionism, on the other hand, sees the nation of Israel above all as a deadly threat to world peace and the international order.[20]

The UN Special Rapporteur on freedom of religion and belief, Ahmed Shaheed, considered this increase in left-wing antisemitism in a recent report which looked specifically at the question of antisemitism:

> Numerous reports of an increase in many countries of 'left-wing' antisemitism, in which individuals claiming to hold anti-racist and anti-imperialist views employ antisemitic narratives or tropes in the course of expressing anger at policies or practices of the Government of Israel. [The Rapporteur] emphasizes that it is never acceptable to render Jews as proxies for the Government of Israel.[21]

Left-wing antisemitism has deep roots in 19th century political thought but its 20th century manifestation is closely linked to the combined forces of identity politics, anti-colonialism, and anti-imperialism unleashed in the 1960s and 1970s. Analysis of the apparent paradox of the emergence of antisemitism on the political left yields a useful insight into how facets of this ancient hatred have evolved and present themselves in a modern guise.

Anti-Zionism: an acceptable face of antisemitism?

The view that the State of Israel should not exist – the basic form of anti-Zionism – has come to form a cornerstone of postmodern left antisemitism. In its more extreme expressions, it denies both the very concept of Jewish peoplehood entitled to self-determination and the right of a lawfully constituted state to safeguard the security of its borders and its people. "Anti-Zionism demonizes, dehumanizes, and delegitimizes Israel in order to bring about its destruction," Melanie Phillips[22] has written.[23]

The idea of the Jewish state itself remains controversial within certain circles of contemporary Jewish thought which advocate a loosening of the ties between faith and nation. Furthermore, it is important to distinguish the pre-Second World War period, when Zionism was just one solution proposed to the Jewish problem among several, from the post-Second World War period, when there was consensus about the existence of the State of Israel amongst an overwhelming majority of Jews, both within Israel and outside.[24]

The most eloquent opponents of Theodore Herzl's 19th century movement promoting modern Jewish nationalism (Zionism) included emancipated and assimilated Jews in Europe and the United States. Amongst their wide-ranging concerns was a fear that establishment of a Jewish nation in Palestine would serve to stamp Jews as strangers in their native countries and undermine their status as citizens of those lands.

Zionism had (and, on the extreme margins of the Ultra-orthodox community, still has) its religious opponents, too. Rabbinical opposition takes different forms but includes the orthodox view that Jewishness is to be defined in terms of religious faith and practice, not in terms of physical place.

Today there are concerns that certain Jewish intellectuals and opinion-formers within Israel are now turning aside from the basic Zionist political demand for recognition of the sovereignty, territorial integrity, and political independence of a Jewish state in at least part of Palestine.

Yoram Hazony[25] has used the term, 'post-Zionism', to describe the period dating from the election of a Labor Prime Minister, Yitzhak Rabin, in 1992, during which, in his view, the idea of the Jewish state has begun to die. Post-Zionism, he argues, is a movement within Israeli culture which no longer sees Israel as a Jewish state but rather as a "state of citizens – a regime that not only seeks a separation between Jewish religion and state but which also seeks a separation between Jewish *nationality* and state" (italics in original).[26]

He is greatly concerned by the rise of post-Zionism and by its implications for the future of the Jewish state. Although the opinions of post-Zionist Jews may be considered anti-Semitic in some quarters, it is more likely that they are attributable to the kind of national existential weariness identified by an Israeli political commentator, Yoel Marcus, in 1995:

> Our people has long since tired of bearing Zionism on its shoulders generation after generation. While the Arabs have remained faithful to their ideology of the holiness of the land, preferring to forgo peace rather than concede anything of their demands, Israel is ready lightly to withdraw from the lands that were the cradle of Judaism in exchange for personal safety and a 'normal' life.[27]

In 2019, notwithstanding concerns expressed about it, post-Zionism remains very much the view of only a small minority in Israel. For the most part, Israelis remain solidly committed to the vision of a Jewish state, even if there is also a desire for more normalcy. In the view of Tzvi Fleischer[28], this commitment only strengthened after the second intifada of 2000-2004 when Israel offered a two-state peace: "since then most Israelis came to regard the sorts of views expressed by Marcus in 1995 as hopelessly naive or impractical."[29]

Anti-Zionism and the postmodern Left

Support for creation of the State of Israel was widespread on the political left during the 1947-48 Arab-Israeli war. The Six-Day War in 1967, however, marked a specific turning point in international perceptions of Israel. After 1967, the opposition to Israel which came from the left was directed at its occupation of territory, especially the West Bank, its military strength, and its perceived status as a hegemonic regional power closely allied with the United States of America.

Soviet criticism of Israel, in turn, fed a fervent communist anti-Zionism which promoted defamatory theories of a global conspiracy funded by Jewish money committed to wreaking political and economic havoc in Western countries.

When the postmodern left began to emerge in the 1950s and 1960s, it absorbed much of this Soviet propaganda about Jews and Israel into its own worldview. A key tenet was, and remains, commitment to anti-Zionism – the view that the State of Israel is illegitimate and should not exist. Added to the anti-Zionist denial of Israel's claim to an ancestral homeland was "a contradictory claim that the Jews sought to maintain a 'racial state' in Israel."[30]

Historically, anti-Zionism has been quite distinct from antisemitism. Whereas the racist prejudice of antisemitism was largely a phenomenon of the political right, anti-Zionism was based on what has been described as "a relatively objective assessment of the prospects for success for some Jews in Israel/Palestine."[31] In recent decades, however, as anti-Zionism has developed into a rejection of the legitimacy of the State of Israel, anti-Zionism and antisemitism have converged.

The anti-Zionism of the postmodern left, however, owes less to the fevered conspiracy theories of the Soviet era. It arises from a determination amongst a generation of people who came of age after the Second World War to oppose racism and colonialism. Israel, according to the postmodern left, is an illegitimate remnant of Western colonialism in the Middle East – a view increasingly endorsed by the United Nations as it added newly decolonized states to its membership.

Anti-Zionists of the postmodern left invariably insist that

their target is neither Jews nor individual Israeli citizens going about their ordinary lives. It is the State of Israel itself which is their target. They hold it to be a political regime promulgating what they believe with conviction to be the illegal, coercive, and dehumanizing treatment of Palestinians. It is a line of argument that attempts to defend the distinction between anti-Jewish remarks and criticism of Israeli government policy.

These trenchant critics of Israel, nevertheless, do not appear to have much concern for alleviating the suffering of Israeli citizens who endure missile and bomb attacks as they go about their 'ordinary lives' within Israel. While there is much to be said for Palestinians, it seems there often appears to be little, if anything, to be said for Israelis. Moral hyperbole is combined with deliberate disinformation to justify attacks on what the anti-Zionists of the postmodern left call the 'political regime' of Israel.

United Nations Resolution 3379: Zionism = Racism

The value of the proposition that Jews sought to secure the racialized status of Israel intensified in 1975 when the United Nations General Assembly passed a resolution declaring Zionism to be "a form of racism and racial discrimination."[32] Rescinded in 1991, its legacy remains potent. On the left it is widely accepted that Zionism, the movement that created Israel, commits the most heinous of the post-colonial world's moral crimes: racism.[33]

As remarked earlier, postmodern left opposition to racism and colonialism – and, thence, to Israel – is also interwoven with a deep-seated hostility to the USA and its allies. Israel, according to this worldview, is a settler, colonial venture which is part of a Western drive to dominate the Middle East region. Dave Rich[34] explains that according to this view: "Zionism is part of a global nexus of power that is white, Western, and wealthy, and Diaspora Jews who support Israel are themselves part of this racist structure."

It is a worldview to which Jeremy Corbyn[35] and others

on the postmodern left are committed: racism is about structural discrimination whereby power is exercised over the marginalized. Since it is axiomatic for these critics that the State of Israel is a racist endeavour, they simply cannot accept that a commitment to anti-racism and defence of the powerless against the claims of the powerful can be antisemitic. If colonialism is racism, it cannot be antisemitic to condemn colonialism.

The step from the idea that Zionism is racism to the idea that Israel as a country should not exist at all is not such a big one. And it is a step many on the political left – in Britain as well as in other countries such as the United States and Australia – have taken. They use the word, 'Zionist', as an epithet to denigrate those who defend Israel. As Rich notes, "this has become a moral question and one of political identity, rather than an objective analysis of Israeli policy."[36]

What is distinctive about this new mutation of a centuries-old hatred is that its ostensible object is the State of Israel itself, not individual Jews or Jewish communities and groups. But it extends to any Jews who demur from the view that Israel is "a diabolical imperialist conspiracy that must be destroyed."[37] This is the vast majority of modern Jews.

Different forms of antisemitism as expressed on the political right, the political left, or in Islamic societies do, of course, overlap. What makes left-wing antisemitism distinctive is its different emphases.

Left-wing antisemitism tends to be expressed in terms of moral imperatives. Its focus is on the alleged capitalist financial depredations of Jews, opposing what it perceives as the supremacist claims of Zionism and the questionable legitimacy of Jewish national consciousness. Furthermore, in alliance with international human rights non-government organisations (NGOs), it adopts the language of human rights as it criticizes Israel's neo-colonial ambitions and campaigns for the liberation of the 'long-oppressed' Palestinian people.[38]

Antisemitism and international human rights: boycott, divestment and sanctions

Opposition to Israel from the political left has now attained a global reach largely because of its association with international human rights groups and NGOs. As Goldhagen has remarked, "the left's antisemitism has merged its long-standing identification of Jews with the predations of capitalism and the world economic order with its newfound relentless international orientation."[39]

The old tropes of classical, racial antisemitism are not features of left-wing antisemitism. It is much more overtly political and secular in its forms. Far from engaging in 'Jew hatred', human rights advocates remain convinced that they are simply upholding fundamental humanitarian principles in their pursuit of international justice and peace. They insist their hostility is not directed to Jewish people, as such, but to their financial depredations and neo-colonial practices which prevent the vulnerable from realizing cherished goals.[40]

Yet the political left's fashionable application of the language of human rights and international justice to criticize actions by the State of Israel amounts to a questioning of the legitimacy of Israel. This questioning, in turn, is characterized by startling inconsistency as standards of extraordinary severity are applied to Israel alone:

> Israel is not condemned for what it does, but for what it is. Syria and Sudan might be criticized for their woeful human rights records, but it is never suggested that either state is illegitimate in itself. Neither state is regarded, in contrast to Israel, as an inherent pariah. Neither state, therefore, is the subject of relentless campaigns questioning their right to exist; nor are they the targets of economic, academic and other boycotts.[41]

As a consequence, Ben Cohen[42] has concluded, "the opposition to Israel's very legitimacy means that the terms 'Jew', 'Israel', and 'Zionist' are increasingly interchangeable in contemporary left-wing discourse."[43]

In other words, the language of humanitarian concern for

rights and justice provides a respectable veil which covers antisemitism. It is a discourse that has given antisemitism "a universal language and justification – that is in tune with the times – for [antisemitic] beliefs and hatreds, albeit transformed and concealed to gain universal appeal."[44] Participants in this discourse within Australia include some trade unions, academics, journalists, political activists, and the Christian churches.

A good example of activism by the Christian churches is what happened at the 7th triennial Forum of the National Council of Churches in Australia (NCCA) in July 2010. At the forum, the NCCA announced that it would "continue to add its voice to the call for an end to Israel's occupation of Palestine."[45]

Declaring its solidarity with Palestinian Christians, the NCCA invited the member churches "to consider a boycott of goods produced by Israeli settlements in the Occupied Palestinian Territories." In a media release, the NCCA said: "It is hoped that such actions will liberate the people [sic] from an experience of injustice to one where a just and definitive peace may be reached."[46]

The call to which the NCCA committed to continue to add its voice was the continuing international Boycott, Divestment and Sanctions (BDS) campaign launched in July 2005 by 171 Palestinian non-governmental organizations in a bid to force Israel to comply with "its obligations under international law".

Questioning Israel's legitimacy

The BDS campaign has a series of three objectives.[47] These objectives, taken together, amount to a sustained attack on the very legitimacy of the State of Israel itself; as such, they warrant closer examination:

1. An end to Israel's occupation and colonization of Arab lands and removal of the Separation Wall

Immediately after the Six-Day War in June 1967, Israel

offered to return much of the land it had captured in exchange for peace. In September 1967, the Arab League responded to Israel's offer by emphatically rejecting it with the three famous 'Nos' of Khartoum: 'no peace with', 'no negotiation with', and 'no recognition of' Israel.

In November 1967, Israel accepted UN Resolution 242 that it should withdraw its forces "from territories occupied in the recent conflict" *as well as* the principle expressed in 242 (1) (ii) of "termination of all claims or states of belligerency and respect for and acknowledgement of the sovereignty of every state in the area and their right to live in peace within secure and recognized boundaries free from threats or acts of force." The Arab states largely rejected 242 at the time, but later tried to reinterpret it as demanding of Israel a unilateral withdrawal to the pre-1967 boundaries.

More than thirty years later, the Separation Wall was erected in response to fears for the security of the Israeli population in the midst of the massive organized terrorist violence of the second Intifada. This onslaught took the form of a campaign of suicide-bombing which, "as every poll among Palestinians has shown, were, and remain, immensely popular."[48]

The first BDS objective appears to date Israel's occupation of Arab lands from 1967, meaning that the lands have been colonized for 53 years. However, when Palestinian negotiator, Nabil Shaath, was interviewed on ABC TV's *Lateline* on 26 September 2011, he declared that Israel "has been in full occupation of our country for years, 62 years." In other words, he dated the occupation from 1949. This suggests that Mr Shaath regards Israel's very existence, not just its occupation of the West Bank, as illegitimate.[49]

2. Equal rights for Arab-Palestinian citizens inside Israel

It is widely, yet quite incorrectly, claimed that Israel is practising a form of *apartheid* – a charge to which figures such as former US President Jimmy Carter and Bishop Desmond Tutu have given weight: "I have been to the Occupied

Palestinian Territory," Tutu wrote in a letter to student protestors at UC Berkeley in California in March 2010, "and I have witnessed the racially segregated roads and housing that reminded me so much of the conditions we experienced in South Africa under the racist system of Apartheid."[50]

The accusation that Israel is practising a form of apartheid is wholly unfounded. On the contrary, as Cohen has noted, "the only Arabs in the Middle East who enjoy human and civil rights which conform to democratic standards are those who are citizens of Israel."[51] Whereas Palestinian leaders argue that accepting Israel as a Jewish state would mean jeopardizing the status of the country's Arab minority, other commentators hold that "there is no conceptual contradiction between Israel as a Jewish state and as a democracy – the two essential elements of its identity as defined by its Declaration of Independence."[52]

It is true that Palestinians living in the territories do not have the same civil and legal rights as Israeli citizens. The reason is that they are not Israeli citizens. Within Israel, Arab citizens enjoy the same civil, legal and political rights as Jewish citizens. There are Israeli Arab members of the Knesset (the parliament), the army and the police force. Israeli Arabs attend Israeli universities and receive medical treatment in hospitals alongside Israeli Jews. Even so, there are commentators who concede that "it can be reasonably argued that there is social and economic discrimination against Israeli Arabs."[53]

The American feminist, Phyllis Chesler[54], who has passionately attacked the demonization of Israel, has also been very critical of the Israeli government's failure to address the social and economic disparities between sectors of the population:

> Although Israeli Palestinian Arabs may privately admit that their lives as second-class citizens in Israel are far better than the lives of their counterparts all over the Arab world, they remain second-class citizens in Israel proper. Israeli Arabs were not granted equal citizenship [when

choosing to remain in Israel after the 1948 war]. This is
unforgivable, an understandable but huge mistake.[55]

Since Chesler wrote thus in 2003, Israel has done much to
rectify these disparaties and to maximize opportunities for
Israeli Arabs to participate with greater equality in Israeli
society. Legitimate criticism such as this, however, hardly
warrants the charge that Israel is an *apartheid* state for, under
apartheid in South Africa, there was a systematic separation of
races and the areas they were permitted to occupy. Bernard
Harrison[56] pointedly contends:

> Israel stands virtually alone in the world, among nations
> facing an immediate military threat to their existence in
> its willingness to countenance within its borders, neither
> interning nor expelling its members, a large population
> of people sharing the culture and religion of her declared
> enemies.[57]

*3. The right of return of Palestinian refugees as set out in United
Nations Resolution 194*

Instead of accepting the two-state solution proposed by
the United Nations in 1947, the Arab-Palestinian side rejected
it and opted for violence. The eruption of war led directly to
the refugee crisis as hundreds of thousands of Palestinian
Arabs fled the fighting. According to UN figures, 650,000
Arab inhabitants of mandatory Palestine fled the fighting.[58]

The historical account of what happened has been highly
politicized. Most Palestinians fleeing the fighting were
probably sympathetic to the aggressors and many joined
the fighting. Some appear to have been driven out by Israeli
forces. Palestinian propaganda also had a part to play. Yet
most who fled simply did so to get out of harm's way. The
difficulty is that they found themselves on the losing side
of the war. Once hostilities came to an end, the Palestinian
refugees were not allowed back.

The majority of the 750,000 Jewish refugees forced to
flee Arab countries were resettled in Israel. By contrast, the
Arab countries refused to resettle or grant citizenship to the

Palestinian refugees, promised them they would be able to return to their former homes, and, pending re-conquest of Israel, preferred to keep them in refugee camps which exist to this day.

The United Nations General Assembly (UNGA) passed Resolution 194 in December 1948. It stated that refugees "wishing to return to their homes and live at peace with their neighbours should be permitted to do so at the earliest practicable date."[59] Resolutions of the UN General Assembly are not binding, unlike those of the Security Council, so the status of the claimed *right* of return is open to question. Yet even if there is a *right* of return, Resolution 194 explicitly states that it is conditional upon a willingness to live peacefully. As Robin Shepherd[60] has observed:

> Since Israel had every reason to believe that the refugees did *not* want to 'live at peace with their neighbours', it is at least arguable that they forfeited their right to return. Which other state in the world could reasonably be asked to welcome back hundreds of thousands of people who had been taught by their leaders to strive for that state's destruction?[61]

Furthermore, the 'right of return' contained within UNGA Resolution 194 was in the context of a larger peace proposal recommended in that resolution which consisted of fifteen articles and covered matters such as management of the Holy Places in Israel and the establishment of a Conciliation Commission. No one has ever suggested reviving the many other aspects of that proposal other than refugee return.[62]

However, the Arab-Palestinian leadership presses for the right of return for another reason. Arab leaders have always been candid that any return of Palestinian refugees would not be as a minority group but as a *majority* group so as to eliminate the Jewish state and live in a Muslim state.

Alan Dershowitz[63] cites the secretary of the Arab Higher Command, Emile Ghoury, who, in August 1948, told the *Beirut Telegraph* that "it is inconceivable that the refugees should be sent back to their homes while they are occupied by the Jews. It would serve as a first step toward their recognition of Israel."[64] A two-state solution would no longer be possible if UNGA Resolution 194 were to be implemented. By calling for implementation of UNGA Resolution 194 as its third objective, the BDS campaign effectively declares itself in favour of a one-state solution.

BDS: justice for whom?

The BDS campaign holds a particular view of the situation in Israel which makes mention neither of Arab aggression against Israel in 1948 or 1967; nor of the Palestinian rejection in 2000-01 of the Clinton-Barak offer of a Palestinian state in the West Bank and Gaza, including removal of Jewish settlements (often cited as a barrier to peace); nor of the more generous offer of statehood (which included an offer to withdraw from 93 per cent of the West Bank) made by Prime Minister Ehud Olmert in 2008; nor of the enduring commitment of Hamas to destruction of the state of Israel.

In short, the BDS campaign perpetuates the idea of Palestinian victimhood described with some perspicacity by the Israeli historian, Benny Morris. Variously described as a 'new' or 'revisionist' historian, Morris has been critical both of Israel and of Zionism, and today adopts a more hawkish position:

> One of the characteristics of the Palestinian national movement has been the Palestinians' view of themselves as perpetual victims of others – Ottoman Turks, British officials, Zionists, Americans – and never to appreciate that they are, at least in large part, victims of their own mistakes and iniquities. In the Palestinian *Weltanschauung*, they never set a foot wrong; their misfortunes are always the fault of others.[65]

This experience of victimhood is captured in each of the three objectives of the BDS campaign. Furthermore, and notwithstanding the claim that "the focus of BDS is on Israel's abuse of power and Israeli institutions that acquiesce in that power, not on Jewish people or Judaism,"[66] a closer examination of each of the campaign's objectives shows that the BDS is not, in fact, presenting a nuanced critique of Israeli government policy at all.

Many thoughtful and well-meaning supporters of the BDS in Australia would no doubt insist that their only purpose is to campaign for justice for the Palestinians. Some of these people would be genuinely distressed by an accusation of anti-Semitism. They would insist that they do not hate Jews; they simply hate injustice.

Furthermore, such BDS supporters may well insist that they are not attacking Israel but simply criticizing policies of its government. Although there is a tendency amongst critics of Israel to assert that Judaism is merely confessional and that claims for the territorial boundaries of a state are both recent and illegitimate, "modern Jewish identity increasingly embraces cultural, religious and national elements."[67]

Yet examination of the three objectives of BDS indicates that the campaign has a darker purpose: to damage and delegitimize the Jewish state by calling into question the basis of its creation and continued existence as a liberal democracy.

Critics respond to this by noting that questions about the legitimacy of the state of Israel are being raised not only by non-Jewish critics but also by Jews – both Israeli and non-Israeli - themselves. But this line of argument fails to recognize the fallacy of what Dershowitz calls "argument by ethnic admission", the fallacious reasoning being to conclude "that one side of a dispute must be right if some people who are ethnically identified with *that* side support the *other* side" (italics in original).[68]

The discourse of de-legitimization is anti-Semitic. If one participates in this discourse and shares the objectives of those who propound the discourse, it is not open to claim to be untainted by their ideological position. By allying oneself with a position or an argument that is anti-Semitic, one becomes a participant in anti-Semitic discourse. To argue otherwise is disingenuous.

Jeremy Corbyn and the antisemitism of the postmodern Left

Perhaps the most prominent contemporary example of left-wing antisemitism is provided by the British Labour Party. The latent – and now blatant – antisemitism that has seeped through its ranks into the public domain over the last four or five years has been one of the most divisive issues to confront Labour. Responsibility for this crisis can be set at the feet of the party's leader, Jeremy Corbyn, whom the party elected as leader in September 2015; he had been a member of the House of Commons since 1983 but had never held ministerial office nor had a place on the party's front bench.

Until then, Corbyn had been a fringe member of the party devoting much of his time to attending protests and speaking at rallies denouncing the United States, NATO, Israel, and even his own country. Corbyn has been a noted apologist for tyranny, publicly offering his support to Libya's Colonel Gaddafi, the Castro regime in Cuba, and to Hamas, the ruler of Gaza. Corbyn has also been a consistent critic of Israel and its successive governments, and a long-term supporter of the Labour Movement Campaign for Palestine which adopted a policy of installing a democratic secular state to replace Israel.[69]

How is it that the political left, so long associated with notions of economic justice, fairness and equality, could become the conduit for such blatant prejudice and discrimination levelled against Jewish people?

One view is that Corbyn is a product of a political culture whose deep roots can be traced back to the 19th century when Marxism posed what became known as 'the Jewish Question' – a questioning of the economic and political status of Jews in European society. This evolved into the overt antisemitism prosecuted by the Soviet Union in the 20th century which included pogroms and purges, anti-Zionist propaganda, and allegations of Jewish disloyalty.

After Corbyn's election as leader stories about antisemitism and anti-Zionism within the Labour Party started to appear with increasing frequency. Accounts of antisemitic incidents at university Labour clubs emerged as well as news of suspensions of some party members for alleged antisemitic language.[70] As a mounting crisis of antisemitism engulfed Labour, and while Jewish support for the Labour Party collapsed, Corbyn appeared reluctant to acknowledge the existence of any problem.

Corbyn did establish an inquiry into antisemitism within the party which gathered evidence selectively and delivered its report – which cleared the party of any wrong-doing – very quickly.[71] The chair of the inquiry, Sharmishta Chakrabarti, a human rights lawyer, was subsequently compromised when she joined the Labour Party and was nominated by Corbyn to sit as a Labour peer in the House of Lords.

The problem of antisemitism within Labour's ranks did not disappear, however. Indeed, it became more acute early in 2019 with the resignation of Labour MPs such as Luciana Berger, and the suspension of another, Chris Williamson, for remarks he made about antisemitism.[72]

Later in 2019, Berger's resignation was followed by that of Louise Ellman who was reported to have said of Corbyn, "I see no indication at all that he recognizes his responsibility for what is happening, or indeed wants to do anything about it. I see no contrition, no recognition of his role in this terrible situation."[73]

Another Labour MP, John Mann, who is not Jewish, also resigned in 2019 citing Corbyn's repeated failure to act against antisemitism. Mann, who served until his resignation as Chairman of the All-Party Parliamentary Group on Antisemitism, warned that "[Corbyn] has given a green light to anti-Semites and done nothing to reverse that."[74] Since leaving Parliament, Mann has been appointed as Independent Adviser to the UK Government on Antisemitism.

Postmodern left antisemitism has become front-page news because of this blatant manifestation within the British

Labour Party. Corbyn, himself, was not responsible for this antisemitism; but his failure to address antisemitism brought the party to the point where even its supporters believe the party to be systemically antisemitic. As Adam Wagner, a Labour barrister, has remarked:

> When people look back on Labour and Jeremy Corbyn's response to antisemitism, the question is unlikely to be whether the party became institutionally antisemitic, but when. Taken together, the failures in leadership, processes and culture have created a toxic brew. For a party with a history of being at the vanguard of anti-racism, it hurts.[75]

Dave Rich, whose seminal work on Left-wing antisemitism in Britain has helped to identify the depth and complexity of the problem, has supported this view. Rich argues that Corbyn's responses to the issue of antisemitism revealed "a pattern of thought and behaviour that speaks to a deeper malaise that has been building within the British left for decades. It reflects an antisemitic political culture."[76]

Whereas the crisis about antisemitism currently engulfing the British Labour Party has focused, to a large extent, on the behaviour of Corbyn himself, Labour's problem is that of institutional antisemitism. Not every party member is antisemitic; but the themes of anti-racism, anti-colonialism, anti-capitalism, and anti-Zionism have all combined to provide fertile ground in which antisemitic attitudes have grown and festered within the British Labour Party.

Yet Corbyn refused to concede – let alone address – the existence of antisemitism within Labour ranks because he refused to accept that opposition to racist colonialism is equivalent, in the case of Israel, to Jew hatred.[77]

According to the world view to which he is committed, racism is about structural discrimination whereby power is exercised over the marginalized. Since it is axiomatic for these critics that the State of Israel is a racist endeavour, they simply cannot accept that a commitment to anti-racism and defence of the powerless against the claims of the powerful can be antisemitic. If colonialism is racism, it cannot be antisemitic to condemn colonialism.

Scarcely a week goes by without news emerging of some new convulsion gripping the party.[78] In Rich's view, "this combination of ideological hostility, personal prejudice, and organizational failings has brought Jeremy Corbyn's Labour Party to a state that can be fairly described as institutionally antisemitic."[79]

As Labour's scandal of antisemitism deepens, many Jewish leaders in the UK now consider the party – long the home of British Jewry – a threat to Jewish life in that country. According to a poll commissioned by the London-based *Jewish Chronicle* in September 2018, 85.6 per cent of British Jews consider antisemitism to have significantly infiltrated all levels of the Labour Party.[80]

The Squad: postmodern Left antisemitism in the United States

The cultural shift in emphasis that has occurred in left-wing politics in the United Kingdom has also taken place in the United States. As in Britain, identity politics in the USA is driving a determination to correct perceived imbalances of power expressed in questions of race, gender, and intersectionality.

Amongst a younger generation of political activists on the American left, these progressive issues have displaced concerns about economic injustice; but they have also inflamed postmodern forms of antisemitism.

The confluence of Islam and the politics of identity has been particularly powerful in driving antisemitism on the American political left where contempt for the United States has comingled with a rejection of Israel, which is considered one part of the bitter legacy of Western imperialism in the Middle East. The enthusiastic support shown for Israel and for Jews by President Trump serves only to fuel postmodern antisemitism on the American left.

Four first-term members of Congress have quickly become the focus concern about this rise of postmodern antisemitism in the United States. Alexandria Ocasio-Cortez, Ilhan Omar, Rashida Tlaib, and Ayanna Pressley were all elected to the House of Representatives at the mid-term elections in November 2018. The four Congresswomen have been dubbed 'The Squad', a term coined by Ocasio-Cortez one week after their election victories.[81]

All four Congresswomen – but Omar and Tlaib, in particular – have attracted severe rebukes for repeatedly invoking antisemitic stereotypes about the dual loyalty of Jews, the economic power of Jews, and Israel's colonial intentions.[82]

Criticism of Israel, in particular, became the focus of a row with the Israeli government in August 2019 when Omar and Tlaib were denied entry to Israel on the basis of their overt support for the BDS campaign. In making its decision to deny them entry, there were reports that the Israeli government came under pressure from President Trump to make its decision.[83] However, when Israel subsequently granted Tlaib permission to visit the country subject to the condition that she did not express any political views, the Congresswoman declined the invitation.[84]

There are growing concerns that by tolerating, and even excusing, the antisemitism expressed by the Squad, the Democratic Party is institutionalizing antisemitism in much the same way that the Labour Party in Britain has done.[85] And it is likely that left-wing antisemitism in the United States, as in Britain, is only set to worsen. As Victor Davis Hanson[86] has remarked:

> Radical Muslims and the Left disguise their hatred of Jews by claiming that they are only championing downtrodden Palestinians. Anti-Semitism is only going to intensify. It is naturally at home on the multicultural Left. The media, popular culture, universities, and left-wing political parties either cannot or will not stop it.[87]

Is there a problem of postmodern Left antisemitism in Australia?

The antisemitism found in the Labour Party in Britain and the Democratic Party in the United States are not isolated instances of Left-wing antisemitism. Although the graffiti that marred the 2019 Australian federal election campaign bore many of the tropes of right-wing antisemitism, it is clear that antisemitic views are now also being expressed more frequently on the political left in Australia.

For the most part, the Australian Labor Party has been spared the travails of either its British counterpart or the Democratic Party in the USA. However, voices critical of Israel, and suspicious of supposed Jewish influence in finance, politics, and the media, are becoming increasingly prominent on the political left in Australia.

In her 2018 report on antisemitism in Australia for the Executive Council of Australian Jewry, Julie Nathan catalogued comments – and responses posted on social media to such comments – made by people on the political right, such as the senator, Fraser Anning (United Australia Party, Qld), and Clive Palmer. But the report also recorded numerous remarks and responses made by others on the political left such as NSW ALP MP Shaoquett Moselmane, former NSW Premier Bob Carr, and NSW Greens MP Tamara Smith.[88] These remarks tended to focus on support for the Palestinians and criticism of the State of Israel.

Carr's remarks, in particular, have caused considerable dismay in some quarters because of his earlier, public support for Israel and the Jewish community in Australia.[89] His views had changed by the time he ceased serving as Foreign Minister in the Gillard Government when he became very critical of what he called the "pro-Israel lobby in Melbourne" which had "extremely conservative instincts" and which wielded disproportionate influence over government policy.[90]

But his change of view, and the rise of left wing antisemitism in Australia in general, can be explained by the politics of those Labor-held seats which now contain large Muslim populations that are religiously and culturally conservative but that are also hostile to Israel and sympathetic to the Palestinian cause.

Such factors help to explain why Labor has been pulled further away from its historically pro-Zionist position to utter denunciations of not just the Israeli government but the State of Israel itself. A critical feature of postmodern left antisemitism is the revival of anti-Zionist rhetoric fueled by its antagonism to the existence of Israel, "a prosperous democracy and undeclared nuclear power that is nearing the historic threshold of being home to the majority of the world's Jews."[91]

The Australian Greens frequently display similar hostility to Israel. Its stance on Israel and Palestine is marked by the kind of anti-Zionism so characteristic of postmodern left antisemitism. In a tweet published on 8 June 2018, Mehreen Faruqi, the Greens Senator for NSW, declared: "Thanks everyone for standing in solidarity with the Palestinian people. End the occupation. End the blockade. Free Palestine!"[92] There is every indication that the Greens' anti-Zionism will not diminish but only intensify.[93]

There are, indeed, few signs that left wing positions on Israel, Zionism, and antisemitism are likely to change quickly, either in Australia or the UK. As Philip Mendes[94] has noted, "Left groups do not view Jews as a vulnerable or oppressed group, and do not prioritize the struggle against anti-Semitism."[95]

At the same time, nor are Jews as vulnerable as they once were to oppression from right wing regimes that served to rally the support of the left. Yet a vital opportunity now presents itself to the ALP and other groups on the left of Australian politics to ensure that the long-standing commitment of the Australian left to pursuit of justice and human decency remains free of the ugly taint of antisemitism.

REFERENCES

1 Melanie Phillips, *The World Turned Upside Down: The Global Battle over God, Truth, and Power* (New York: Encounter Books, 2010), 196.

2 Julie Nathan, "The resurgence of racism in the 2019 federal election – a deep and disturbing trend", ABC Religion & Ethics (31 May 2019).

3 Sophie Deutsch, "Leeser: 'Dirtiest, nastiest election I can remember'", *Australian Jewish News* (30 May 2019).

4 Jeremy Jones, Anti-Semitism in Australia 2010, (Sydney: ECAJ, 2010), p.6. The report is prepared annually on behalf of the Executive Council of Australian Jewry to assist in the understanding of anti-Jewish prejudice in contemporary Australia.

5 Jeremy Jones, as above, 9.

6 Julie Nathan, Report on Antisemitism in Australia 2018 (Sydney: ECAJ, 2018), 7.

7 Deborah Lipstadt (b. 1947) is an American historian and Professor of Modern Jewish History and Holocaust Studies at Emory University in the USA.

8 Deborah Lipstadt, *Antisemitism Here and Now* (Melbourne, VIC: Scribe, 2019), 24.

9 International Holocaust Remembrance Alliance, "Spelling of antisemitism".

10 International Holocaust Remembrance Alliance, Working Definition of Antisemitism (26 May 2016).

11 Daniel Jonah Goldhagen, *The Devil that Never Dies: The Rise and Threat of Global Antisemitism* (New York: Little, Brown & Co., 2013), 81.

12 Jonathan Sacks (b. 1948), a British Orthodox rabbi, theologian, and writer, was Chief Rabbi of the United Hebrew Congregations of the Commonwealth from 1991 to 2013.

13 Jonathan Sacks, quoted in Bernard Harrison, *The Resurgence of Anti-Semitism: Jews, Israel, and Liberal Opinion* (Lanham, Maryland: Rowman & Littlefield, 2006), 20.

14 Marc Thiessen, "The rise of anti-Semitism on the Left", *Philadelphia Inquirer* (13 August 2019).

15 Israel's Religiously Divided Society, Pew Research Center (March 2016), 222-223.

16 Daniel Jonah Goldhagen (b.1959) is an American historian noted for studies of Nazism and the Holocaust.

17 Daniel Jonah Goldhagen, as above, 175.

18 See Deborah Lipstadt, as above, 19.

19 Robert Wistrich (1945-2015), a leading scholar of antisemitism, was head

of the Vidal Sassoon International Centre for the Study of Antisemitism at the Hebrew University of Jerusalem.

20 Robert Wistrich, "The Changing Face of Anti-Semitism", *Commentary*, March 2013, Vol. 135 (3), 31-34, 33.

21 *Combatting Antisemitism*, as above, para. 17.

22 Melanie Phillips (b.1951), a British journalist, is noted for commentary about antisemitism.

23 See Melanie Phillips, https://www.facebook.com

24 I am grateful to Dr Tzvi Fleischer for making this point clear to me.

25 Yoram Hazony (b. 1969) an Israeli philosopher and political theorist, is President of the Herzel Institute in Jerusalem and author of The Virtue of Nationalism (2018).

26 Yoram Hazony, *The Jewish State: The Struggle for Israel's Soul* (New York: Basic Books, 2000), xxv.

27 Cited in Yoram Hazony, as above, 71.

28 Tzvi Fleischer, is based at the Australia/Israel & Jewish Affairs Council.

29 Tzvi Fleischer, private email correspondence with the author (4 October 2019).

30 David Cesarani, "Anti-Zionism in Britain, 1922-2002: Continuities and Discontinuities", *The Journal of Israeli History*, Vol. 25, No. 1 (March 2006), 131-160, 146.

31 Philip Mendes, "When does criticism of Zionism and Israel become anti-Jewish racial hatred?", in Peter Kurti (ed.), *What's New with Anti-Semitism?* (Centre for Independent Studies: St Leonards, NSW, 2012), 15.

32 United Nations General Assembly Resolution 3379 was passed on 10 November 1975 by a vote of 72 to 35, with 32 abstentions. It was revoked on 16 December 1991 by UN General Assembly Resolution 46/86 by a vote of 111 to 25, with 13 abstentions.

33 Dave Rich, *The Left's Jewish Problem: Jeremy Corbyn, Israel and Antisemitism* (Biteback Publishing: London, 2018), 112.

34 Dave Rich, a British historian and commentator, is head of policy at Community Security Trust in the UK.

35 Jeremy Corbyn (b. 1949) is a British politician who was leader of the British Labour Party and Leader of the Opposition from 2015 until 2020, including general elections in 2017 and 2019.

36 Dave Rich, *The Left's Jewish Problem*, as above, 343.

37 Robert Wistrich, as above, 32.

38 Daniel Jonah Goldhagen, as above, 250.

39 Daniel Jonah Goldhagen, as above, 246.

40 Daniel Jonah Goldhagen, as above, 250, 388.

41 Ben Cohen, "A Discourse of delegitimisation: The British Left and the Jews", originally written for the Institute of Jewish Policy Research, London, 2003, 3.

42 Ben Cohen, a journalist based in New York, writes about Jewish affairs and Middle Eastern politics for the Jewish News Syndicate.

43 Ben Cohen, as above, 3.

44 Daniel Jonah Goldhagen, as above, 399.

45 The National Council of Churches in Australia, founded in 1994, is an ecumenical organization bringing together some 19 member churches for the purposes of dialogue, practical cooperation, and political lobbying. In its time, the Executive Body of the NCCA has issued social justice policy statements on issues such as gambling, poverty, housing and racism.

46 See http://www.ncca.org.au

47 See http://www.bdsmovement.net

48 Benny Morris, *One State, Two States* (New Haven: Yale University Press, 2009), 180.

49 "Saying too much", *Australia/Israel Review*, Vol.36 No.11, November 2011, p.37.

50 Desmond Tutu, quoted in Sonja Karkar, *Boycott, Divestment and Sanctions: A Global Campaign to End Israeli Apartheid* (Melbourne: Australians for Palestine, 2011), 5.

51 Ben Cohen, as above 4.

52 Yossi Klein Halevi, "The real obstacle to Palestinian statehood", *The Globe and Mail* (Toronto), October 7, 2011.

53 Melanie Phillips, *The World Turned Upside Down: The Global Battle Over God, Truth and Power* (New York: Encounter, 2010), 66.

54 Phyllis Chesler (b. 1940), an American writer and psychotherapist, is based at the College of Staten Island (CUNY) in New York.

55 Phyllis Chesler, *The New Anti-Semitism: The Current Crisis and What We Must Do About It* (New York: Jossey-Bass, 2003), p.165.

56 Bernard Harrison is Emeritus Professor of Philosophy at the University of Utah and the author of *The Resurgence of Anti-Semitism: Jews, Israel and Liberal Opinion,* published in 2006.

57 Bernard Harrison, *The Resurgence of Anti-Semitism: Jews, Israel and Liberal Opinion* (Maryland: Rowman & Littlefield, 2006), p. 133.

58 Comparable estimates put the number of Jewish refugees expelled from neighbouring Arab countries during the post-1948 years at 850,000.

59 UN General Assembly Resolution 194, para. 11.

60 Robin Shepherd (b. 1968) is a British political analyist and commentator based at the Halifax International Security Forum.

61 Robin Shepherd, *A State Beyond the Pale: Europe's Problem with Israel* (London: Weidenfeld & Nicolson, 2009) Kindle edition, p. 28.

62 I am grateful to Tzvi Fleischer for making this point to me in private email correspondence (4 October 2019).

63 Alan Dershowitz (b. 1938) is an American lawyer and academic based at Harvard Law School who is a prominent commentator on Israeli and Middle Eastern politics.

64 Alan Dershowitz, *The Case for Israel* (Hoboken, NJ: John Wiley & Sons, 2003), p. 85.

65 Benny Morris, "Rejection", *New Republic* (April 21-28, 2003), 37.

66 Sonja Karkar, *Boycott, Divestment, Sanctions – A Global Campaign to End Israeli Apartheid* (Melbourne: Australians for Palestine, 2011), 39.

67 Ben Cohen, as above, 3.

68 Alan Dershowitz, as above, 221.

69 David Abulafia, "In Corbyn's mind, there is no place for the Jews", *Standpoint* (October 2018), 20-25.

70 See, for example, Aftab Ali, "Oxford University Labour Club students did engage in anti-Semitic behaviour, report finds", *The Independent* (3 August 2016).

71 "Chakrabarti inquiry: Labour not overrun by anti-Semitism", BBC News, (30 June 2016).

72 See, for example, Peter Mason, "The resignation of Luciana Berger is a watershed moment for many Jewish Labour members", *New Statesman*, (20 February 2019); and "MP Chris Williamson loses anti-Semitism suspension appeal", BBC News (10 October 2019).

73 Henry Zeffman, "MP Louise Ellman quits Labour and says Corbyn is a danger to Britain", *The Times*, (16 October 2019).

74 Naomi Levin, "Mann's mission to fight antisemitism", Australia/Jewish Affairs Council (3 October 2019).

75 Adam Wagner, "Labour's antisemitism problem is institutional. It needs investigation", *The Guardian* (8 March 2019).

76 Dave Rich, "The Etiology of Antisemitism in Corbyn's Labour Party", *Israel Journal of Foreign Affairs,* Vol. 12, No. 3 (2018), 357-365, 359.

77 See Daniel Johnson, "Corbyn waves the flag of anti-Semitism", *Standpoint* (December 2018-January 2019), 64-67.

78 See, for example, Harry Cole, "Jeremy Corbyn in fresh anti-Semitism row after defending controversial hard-Left candidate who described Israel as 'a pig'", *Daily Mail* (27 October 2019).

79 Dave Rich, "The Etiology of Antisemitism in Corbyn's Labour Party", as above, 364.

80 Daniel Sugarman, "More than 85 per cent of British Jews think Jeremy Corbyn is antisemitic", *Jewish Chronicle* (13 September 2018).

81 See "The Squad (United States Congress", Wikipedia.

82 See, for example, Ayaan Hirsi Ali, "Can Ilhan Omar overcome her prejudice?", *Wall Street Journal* (12 July 2019).

83 "Benjamin Netanyahu bans Ilhan Omar and Rashida Tlaib from Israel after pressure from Donald Trump", ABC News (16 August 2019).

84 Oliver Holmes, "Rashida Tlaib rejects Israel's offer for 'humanitarian' visit to West Bank", *The Guardian* (16 August 2019).

85 See, for example, Abraham Miller, "Institutionalizing Anti-Semitism in the Halls of Congress", *The American Spectator* (7 March 2019).

86 Victor Davis Hanson (b. 1953), an American classicist and military historian, is based at the Hoover Institution in California.

87 Victor Davis Hanson, "Why Progressive Anti-Semitism – and Why Now?" *National Review* (7 May 2019).

88 See Julie Nathan, Report on Antisemitism in Australia 2018 (Sydney: ECAJ, 2018), 83-100.

89 Nick Dyrenfurth, "British Labour, anti-Semitism and the immorality of Jeremy Corbyn", ABC Religion & Ethics (28 February 2019).

90 "Former foreign minister Bob Carr says 'pro-Israel lobby' influenced government policy", ABC News (10 April 2014).

91 Yaroslav Trofimov, "The New Anti-Semitism", *Wall Street Journal* (12 July 2019).

92 See twitter.com/MehreenFaruqi/status/1005288784869523456

93 Naomi Levin, "Greens problems with Israel and Jews worsen", Australia/Israel & Jewish Affairs Council (29 April 2019).

94 Philip Mendes (b. 1964), Professor of Social Work at Monash University, Victoria, comments frequently on Australian Jewish affairs and Israeli politics.

95 Philip Mendes, "Whatever happened to the political alliance of the Jews and the Left?", ABC Religion & Ethics (20 June 2018).

Picture Credits

Page 20 JOHN HIRST
Photograph, Australian Catholic University, courtesy of Wikipedia.

Page 30 PAUL KELLY
Photograph, News Corp, used with permission.

Page 34 SENATOR AMANDA STOKER
Photograph, Facebook.

Page 59 CHARLES TAYLOR
Photograph courtesy of Oleksandr Makhanets, Wikipedia.

Page 79 DAVID HILLIARD
Photograph courtesy of David Hilliard.

Page 98 EDWIN JUDGE
Photograph courtesy of Edwin Judge and the Centre for Public Christianity.

Page 100 ROGER SCRUTON
Photograph courtesy of Wikipedia.

Page 105 LARRY SIEDENTOP
Photograph courtesy of Wikipedia.

Page 109 RABBI JONATHAN SACKS
Photograph courtesy of Wikipedia.

Page 117 MARGARET SOMERVILLE
Photograph courtesy of Margaret Somerville.

Page 120 LEON KASS
Photograph courtesy of Wikipedia.

Page 160 SUSAN MENDUS
Photograph courtesy of Susan Mendus and the University of York.

Acknowledgments

Defending religious diversity in a multicultural society has become an increasingly complex challenge for secular liberal democracies. General tolerance of religious opinion ebbs quickly when that opinion conflicts with policies or opinions that have been uninformed by faith traditions and practices. Yet citizens with religious beliefs, living alongside those with none, are entitled to contribute their views in public discourse and debate; and they are entitled to be heard.

The challenge of how to strike a balance between competing points of view held by diverse groups of citizens is, of course, nothing new in a secular society. Indeed, the secular status of the state provides an essential foundation for protections of liberty for all citizens. However, when that secular status, itself, becomes the pretext for excluding religious voices and opinions, commitment to diversity, itself, begins to weaken.

The essays in *Sacred & Profane* represent an attempt to examine this complex but pressing question from a number of angles through the prism of different topics. The book draws on my work in the Culture, Prosperity & Civil Society program at the Centre for Independent Studies (CIS). Although it has long been interested in the contribution religion makes to a liberal and secular society, the CIS is a thoroughly secular organisation with no religious affiliation. I am grateful to Tom Switzer, the Executive Director of CIS, for his continuing encouragement and support.

My work has been shaped by conversations and discussions with many people. Accordingly, I wish to express my gratitude, in alphabetical order, to Renae Barker, Iain Benson, Geoffrey Brennan, Michael Casey, Nick Cater, Simon Cowan, Scott Cowdell, Anthony Daniels, Henry Ergas, Tzvi Fleischer, Robert Forsyth, Neil Foster, Maté Hajba, Ian Harper, Paul Kelly, Clive Kessler, Julian Leeser MP, Ron Manners, Chris Merritt, Michael Oondatje, Paul Oslington, Patrick Parkinson, Daniel Pipes, Michael Quinlan, Colin Rubenstein, Jeremy Sammut, Margaret Somerville, Andrew West, Keith Windschuttle, and Augusto Zimmermann. My colleagues at CIS have readily allowed me to test ideas on them, and have been equally ready with their responses.

Once again, I owe a great debt to John Nethercote, Adjunct Professor at the Australian Catholic University in Canberra, for his thorough editing of the manuscript and for correcting a number of errors. Needless to say, the responsibility for any errors that do remain is mine. Anthony Cappello, my publisher at Connor Court, had confidence in the project and I am grateful for his steady encouragement.

Henry Ergas AO made acute observations about the topics covered here in the course of many conversations. He has conferred a signal honour upon the book by writing the foreword, and I express my gratitude to him for his generous remarks and for his friendship.

My wife, Linda, has borne with me as I have worked out the thoughts and ideas in this book. She has been a wonderful companion, both of heart and mind, without whose support none of this would have eventuated.

Peter Kurti,

Sydney, 28 May 2020

www.ingramcontent.com/pod-product-compliance
Lightning Source LLC
Chambersburg PA
CBHW030328270326
41926CB00010B/1548